Confessions of a
Rogue Missionary

A Memoir by
Henry Rambow

Cover Illustration: Author's "self-portrait" in colored pencil and digital media. The flame of faith has been extinguished, but an afterglow remains.

Contents

Prologue: A Brothel in Beijing 5

Chapter 1: Born Again 14

Chapter 2: Transformed by the Spirit 24

Chapter 3: Einstein, Jesus, and a Girl Named Nellie 32

Chapter 4: Spies for Christ 41

Chapter 5: A Sword and a Stalker 52

Chapter 6: A Crisis of Faith 60

Chapter 7: No Turning Back 72

Chapter 8: A Second First Impression 81

Chapter 9: Teaching the Dead 92

Chapter 10: A Serious Matter 104

Chapter 11: A Lesson in Friendship 118

Chapter 12: A Solemn Vow 132

Chapter 13: Fireworks in the Distance 140

Chapter 14: A Shady Offer ⎯⎯⎯⎯⎯ 154

Chapter 15: Girls ⎯⎯⎯⎯⎯ 164

Chapter 16: Boundaries ⎯⎯⎯⎯⎯ 175

Chapter 17: Fifty Days Apart ⎯⎯⎯⎯⎯ 189

Chapter 18: Love and Hate ⎯⎯⎯⎯⎯ 198

Chapter 19: Rising Doubt ⎯⎯⎯⎯⎯ 207

Chapter 20: Meet the Parents ⎯⎯⎯⎯⎯ 216

Chapter 21: In Pursuit of Stardom ⎯⎯⎯⎯⎯ 226

Chapter 22: A Cat and a Ring ⎯⎯⎯⎯⎯ 235

Chapter 23: A Painful Separation ⎯⎯⎯⎯⎯ 244

Chapter 24: Purification ⎯⎯⎯⎯⎯ 253

Chapter 25: Life Together ⎯⎯⎯⎯⎯ 261

Chapter 26: Tribulation ⎯⎯⎯⎯⎯ 272

Chapter 27: Unborn Again ⎯⎯⎯⎯⎯ 284

Prologue:
A Brothel in Beijing

The brothel had been my students' idea, not mine. The private room we occupied was cramped and dark, the air permeated by a gag-inducing haze of cigarette smoke. Between that and the suffocating vapors from the beer and Moutai liquor that were being consumed, it was a miracle no one had passed out from lack of oxygen, much less alcohol poisoning—though in truth, the party was just beginning.

The girl beside me—let me be blunt here; she was a prostitute—took my hand and slid it around the delicate curve of her lower back. Trying to ignore how good that felt, I sought to focus on the reason I was here in Beijing: to share the Gospel of Christ and save lost souls. My own growing doubts had begun to make me less comfortable with this objective, but I still felt obligated to try.

"Where are you from?" I asked in broken Chinese.

"*Dongbei*," she replied. With each syllable, I felt her warm breath on my ear. *Dongbei* means "The Northeast," a region famed not only for its cold weather and ice sculptures but also for its tall, beautifully pale women. And she was indeed tall and beautiful, with none of the dirty qualities I had imagined went hand-in-hand with women of her profession.

We had to shout to be heard. The volume on the karaoke machine was turned up as high as it would go, and every note felt like an ice pick in my eardrums. On top of that, one of my tone-deaf students was moaning drunkenly into the microphone. His words, which I wouldn't have understood anyway, were smeared together by a tasteless deluge of reverb.

"Ah," I said. "I'm from America."

She nodded as if she had already known this, and I stared back at her stupidly, trying to think of something else to say, something I was *capable* of saying in Chinese that I also *wanted* to say. There wasn't much overlap between the two categories.

"I'm their teacher," I said at last, pointing at the three middle-aged Chinese businessmen whose faces were growing redder and redder as they descended into an ever deeper state of drunkenness while fondling the girls at their sides. Gabe, Evan, and Jeff were the English names they had chosen for themselves.

The girl—I hadn't even bothered to ask her name—smiled and pressed her body more firmly against mine. It seemed as if she really liked me; and although I knew that she was essentially an actress whose income depended strongly on how convincing a performance she could give, I believed I was different in her eyes.

"These girls are crazy!" shouted the only other American in the room. His name was Hudson, and he was my colleague and partner in our evangelistic mission. "She just grabbed my crotch!"

He was pointing at his escort—the girl I had picked for him—who had pursued him several feet along the large, U-shaped couch we all sat on, pinning him against one of our students. She said something in Chinese, and everyone's attention turned to Hudson.

Gabe, the student who had masterminded this fiasco of an evening, leaned over to speak to me. With sharp features framed by wavy black hair, he would have been handsome if his right eye weren't always wandering off to the side on its own. The grin that he wore now was even more impish than usual. He pointed to Hudson.

"She wants to know if he is a real man," he said. Gabe's English was normally atrocious, but for once I understood him; apparently the alcohol had boosted his fluency. "Why doesn't he want her?"

What on earth could I say? I wanted to explain that Hudson and I were motivated by the Christian conviction that we should save ourselves for our future wives. I also wanted to convey that Gabe had misjudged the sort of activity it would be appropriate to treat his foreign teachers to. But between the deafening music and my effort to simplify my words to Gabe's English level, I fell drastically short of communicating these ideas.

"We are Christian," I said, "and because of our religion, we cannot do this."

Gabe stared back at me for a moment and then nodded; but there was no glimmer of true comprehension in his eyes, the good one or the lazy one. He probably would have reacted the same way if I had declared that Hudson and I were gay—which he likely suspected anyway.

Gabe said something to the girl, and she backed away from Hudson, looking displeased. Maybe she didn't like being rejected. Or perhaps she was thinking it would be a wasted evening because her celibate patron wouldn't be requesting further, more lucrative services when the singing was over. But after a while, she perked up and began lavishing her attention on our students. This seemed to make everyone—both Hudson and the students—much happier.

"We should leave soon," Hudson said.

"Yes," I replied.

We discussed briefly the best way to break it to our host that although we appreciated his gracious hospitality, we really couldn't stay any longer. Only, at the moment, Gabe was fully engrossed in conversation—if what they were doing could be called conversation—with the girl on his lap. And anyway, it would be rude to leave *too* soon.

I turned my attention back to my own escort and once again racked my brain for something to say. Finding a spark of inspiration from the just-highlighted awkwardness of our situation and the growing sense that I didn't belong here, I said, "I've never been to this kind of place before."

"I believe it."

We again lapsed into silence, and I leaned back, feeling satisfied to have completed another exchange of dialogue. While thinking about what I might say next, I grazed on peanuts and sunflower seeds.

"Do you like this job?" I asked finally.

"Of course I don't like it!" she said.

I nodded, turning her answer over in my mind. Perhaps this was the opening I'd been looking for—my chance to explain to her that Jesus could give her a new life, that he could rescue her from whatever circumstances she was in, no matter how hopeless they seemed. Never mind that I was no longer sure of this myself; I just wished I knew how to say it in Chinese.

"Would you like to come to church?" I asked.

"Yes," she said.

"Really?"

"Really."

There it was—the victory I'd been hoping for. But what now? Should I offer to pick her up next Sunday morning? Give her directions to the church? I wasn't sure my Chinese was good enough for that. So instead, I slipped her my business card—checking discreetly to make sure none of my students would notice—and told her to call me.

Seeming happy to have been invited to church, she again

took my hand in hers and put my arm around her waist. I smiled, feeling I had accomplished something significant. Maybe some good would come out of this evening after all. Perhaps that was why God had brought us here, and now we could leave.

I turned back to Gabe. With one hand, he had his cell phone pressed to his ear; his other was wrapped around his escort, who was sitting in his lap, tickling him while he tried to talk. When he saw me looking at him, he leaned toward me, pointing at his phone.

"It's my wife!" he shouted over the music.

I stared back at him, and before I could say anything, he thrust the phone into my hands. "Talk to her!" he said.

Reluctantly, I held the phone up to my ear. "Hello?"

Through the earpiece came the sound of a Chinese woman releasing an avalanche of words. There was no doubt in my mind that this was indeed Gabe's wife. I had no idea what she was saying, but one thing was certain: She was not happy. I looked back over at Gabe. He was motioning for me to say something more, but before I could think of anything, she hung up.

"Does your wife know what you're doing now?" Hudson asked, pointing to the girl on Gabe's lap.

"Yes!" Gabe shouted back.

"And she doesn't mind?"

"She always forgives me."

Hudson and I looked at each other. Neither of us knew what to say to that. But we had Gabe's attention now, so I could finally arrange our departure.

"We need to go soon," I yelled over the din.

"Okay," Gabe said.

But the next second, he was again entwined with the girl on his lap, and he appeared to have forgotten I was there. I waited for a minute and then looked back at my own escort. She looked deep in thought. I imagined she was daydreaming about sitting next to me in church.

"What are you thinking?" I asked her.

"Nothing," she said.

"Liar!" I shot back.

This turned out not to be the cleverly playful response I had intended it to be. Not only did I fail to imbue the word with a suitably facetious tone, but I also butchered the pronunciation. The sounds that came out of my mouth were much closer to "book yellow" than "liar." But perhaps that was fortunate, because however idiotic a response "book yellow" might be, it was surely better than calling her a liar. Either way, though, I realized I was exhibiting all the charm of a floating turd in an unflushed toilet.

"You must be thinking *something*," I said, in a desperate attempt to recover.

"No," she replied.

The music continued, loud as ever, but no one was singing anymore.

I looked at Gabe. He was still busy. Then I looked at the other two students, thinking that maybe one of them could help. Evan, too, was busy with a girl on his lap, but Jeff looked too drunk to think straight; so I turned to Evan. His English was much better than Gabe's, and he had always seemed a rather considerate fellow. True, it was tempting to draw negative conclusions about him in light of the fact that he had taken his teachers to a brothel, but I could not deny that he was adhering to the Golden Rule. I leaned toward him and got his attention.

"This is very embarrassing," I said.

I had observed that the word "embarrassing" carried some special significance in China, and I hoped using it at this moment would serve as a tactful indicator to Evan that this was an unacceptable situation. Apparently it had the intended effect, because Evan said something quietly to the other students, and a few minutes later we were preparing to leave.

Blessedly, the karaoke machine was turned off at last. Gabe handed a pair of crisp, hundred-kuai bills to each of the girls, and we left the room. As our escorts walked arm-in-arm with us through the maze of hallways toward the exit, I caught sight of another group of girls darting through a doorway. They were wearing long, shiny black boots and leather bikinis covered with metal spikes, and they carried various implements that looked as if they belonged in a medieval Spanish dungeon. Hudson and I exchanged wide-eyed glances but said nothing.

We walked out the front door toward a taxi that was waiting for us, and I sheepishly waved goodbye to my escort. Then I noticed that only one of our students, Jeff, was leaving with us. Gabe and Evan remained standing at the entrance with their arms around their escorts, watching us leave. When our taxi started moving, they turned around and disappeared nonchalantly back into the building, evidently feeling no shame about making plain what their plans were for the rest of the evening.

Above the now-vacant entrance, an enormous neon sign that would have made a Las Vegas casino proud proclaimed the establishment's name out into the night sky. As I watched the Hollywood Club fade into the distance, it didn't occur to me that leaving a business card with my name on it—and the name of my missionary organization—in a brothel might cause problems for me in the future. I was thinking only about how I might manufacture an opportunity to return and share the Gospel with those poor, nameless prostitutes.

My motives were as pure as the blood of Christ.

1

Born Again

You deserve to go to hell.

There exists within you an inherent evil, a sinful nature, which, unfortunately, you lack the power to overcome. Chief among your offenses is the rejection of your Creator—a rejection that you inherited from your most distant ancestor—and since your Creator is holy and infinite, this rejection constitutes a sin so egregious that only an infinite payment will satisfy his justice.

You have two choices: You can pay the price yourself by burning forever in a lake of fire, or you can place your faith in Jesus, whose death on the cross will serve as a substitutionary atonement, adequate because Jesus himself is holy and infinite. The only reasonable option is the latter; and once you have selected it, you can rest in absolute certainty that after you die, you will spend eternity in direct fellowship with your Creator—which is what he wanted in the first place, because he loves you.

That's the essence of the Gospel, the famous "Good News" at the core of the Christian faith. It is a message that I surely heard as a child—my mother was the daughter of a minister, and I grew up immersed in the church, being taught Bible stories as historical facts—but somehow, I failed to grasp it. I was familiar with the notion that "Jesus died for our sins," but I wasn't sure what it meant. I wasn't aware that I had any sins that warranted the execution of the son of God, and I didn't know what his death actually did for me.

In fact, the role of God himself was unclear to me. I knew that he had created the world and had later done some strange and miraculous things as described in the Bible, and I knew that we went to church to pray to him and worship him. Specifically, it seemed that we were supposed to pray when we or someone close to us was sick or dying. I was vaguely aware that it was a toss-up as to whether our requests would be granted, but as a Christian I was supposed to try anyway. And so, at the age of eleven, when I had my first major health crisis, I prayed.

Gym class had just let out, and I was in the middle school locker room—a place that was already synonymous with hell in my mind ever since a mustachioed seventh grader had stuffed me into a trash can behind the showers just for the fun of it. Now, as I was pulling my shirt on over my head, I felt a sudden lurch inside my chest.

I sat down hard on the splintery wooden bench and pressed my hand over my heart, which was thumping so violently that I thought the people around me might be able to hear it. This wasn't the familiar throb brought on by physical exertion, but a frenetic, arrhythmic fluttering that made me feel as if my heart were scraping against the inside of my rib cage. The taste of copper filled my mouth, and I had an overwhelming urge to cough. More than anything else, though, I felt sheer terror, and a certainty that I was about to die.

After a minute or so, it was over. My heart's rhythm returned to normal, and my breathing slowed. I became aware once more of the students around me, the stench of their sweat, and the cacophony of their voices. Nobody had noticed my little emergency, and I was left wondering whether it had been my imagination. But the taste of copper lingered—and so did the fear.

For a long time, I kept the incident secret, hoping that it would never happen again. But it did—and with increasing frequency. Within a few weeks, it was occurring almost daily. Still I told no one, fearing that medical tests might reveal some fatal condition. As long as I went unexamined, I reasoned, there was a chance that I was fine. But deep down, even without a diagnosis, I remained sure that I was dying.

My fear infected my dreams, and I soon began having night terrors. The scenario that played out in my mind was always the same: I was on death row, and my execution was scheduled for the following day. I would, of course, be going to hell. Several times I wandered into my parents' bedroom trying desperately to tell them that I was about to be put to death—but only nonsense passed my lips. "I'm on day," was one of the sentences I kept repeating.

As time passed, my heart condition only seemed to get worse, and my hold on reality became tenuous. I had trouble distinguishing between dreams and real events. Now, whenever my heart began to flutter, I broke into tears and begged God to heal me.

But my prayers went unanswered.

After some time, it occurred to me that prayer might not be enough. Perhaps I needed to make an offering, a promise, to God. I mulled the idea over and decided to vow that if God would allow me to live to the age of twenty, I would become a minister. I was so terrified, so desperate, that even just nine more years of life seemed a lot to ask.

In the days after speaking the vow, I waited anxiously for something to change. The affliction persisted, though, and I turned at last to my parents instead of God. They took me to a cardiologist, who performed all sorts of tests. When the results came in, he sat us down to announce what he had found. The details were beyond my understanding—something about a nerve and a valve—but he made it clear that the problem was not life-threatening.

"Try drinking less caffeine," he said. "That should reduce the frequency of the palpitations."

I followed the doctor's advice, and sure enough, the episodes began occurring monthly instead of daily. I felt tremendously relieved—and, at the same time, stupid. I wasn't dying, and I never had been. But my vow haunted me nonetheless. Perhaps most people would have dismissed it—surely it would be unfair for God to hold a person accountable for a promise made as a terrified, ignorant child—but as I saw it, such a promise had to be kept no matter what.

In the years that followed, I tried to forget about that promise. I thought very little about religion, and it didn't come up again until I started learning about evolution in my ninth-grade biology class. Our teacher, Ms. Brewer, explained the process of natural selection and presented us with the evidence for evolution: the fossil record, shared DNA among different species, junk DNA, and vestigial organs. I found the subject fascinating.

Then, near the end of the unit, Ms. Brewer did something odd: She put us in groups and had each one research a different creation myth. "We wouldn't be doing this at all," she said, her face tight with bottled frustration, "if the state didn't require it."

The next day, we spent half a period presenting our findings. Trios of lanky, giggling teenagers stood awkwardly in front of the class holding up posters with text and photographs that had been shamelessly lifted from encyclopedia articles about cosmic eggs and the Garden of Eden. Everyone felt the silliness of it.

We then spent the second half of the period reviewing the evidence for evolution once more. When we finished, Ms. Brewer looked out over the class with sympathy in her eyes.

"The evidence is overwhelming," she said. "Evolution really is how we got here."

Her sympathy mystified me, and I had no idea why the state of Texas might require us to study creation myths. No one had ever told me that evolution was a controversial topic. I had enjoyed studying it, and I found it to be not just convincing but deeply satisfying. So it surprised me to learn that not everyone felt that way. During lunch, one of my classmates, a guy named Clay, decided to take a stand.

"I don't believe in evolution," he said.

I nearly choked on a half-chewed bite of my peanut-butter-and-jelly sandwich. "Why?" I asked.

"It contradicts the Bible," he said.

Again, I was shocked. Why on earth should we *care* whether it contradicted the Bible? I asked as much, and we began arguing. The exchange ended up lasting several days. Neither of us shifted our position, but in the end, Clay stopped talking about evolution and tried something different.

"You're a sinner," he said. "You need Jesus."

This ignited a whole new argument that culminated in a debate over whether stealing a pencil was as bad as murdering somebody. In Clay's eyes, the two offenses were equivalent because any sin at all—no matter how trivial—had the same effect: It separated you from God.

"That's what sin is," he said. "It's separation from God."

This had a profound effect on me. It was the first time I had heard such a definition of sin. I listened as Clay explained that even though I was a good person by human standards, whatever flaws I had were still significant enough to cut me off from God. In other words, I was bound for hell. The need to accept Christ as my savior was urgent.

When I got home, I shared all of this with my father. That in itself was unusual, because I was the prototypical kid who never had much to say about what happened in school. Furthermore, even though we had always gone to church and my dad said grace before dinner every night, we had never once talked about religion as far as I could remember. I wondered whether he had heard this strange message before. Was it something he believed but had just never explained to me? When I had laid out everything that Clay said, I watched to see how my dad would respond.

"Oh," he said, waving a hand dismissively. "That's what Baptists believe."

I stared at him, waiting for more, but he seemed to have felt that he had said enough. He apparently didn't see a need to explain why we, as Methodists, didn't believe it, or why something that Baptists believed ought to be dismissed automatically. Perhaps if he had clarified why he rejected the message, I would have formulated a clear reason for rejecting it myself. But he didn't, and I didn't.

At school, my debate with Clay continued. I was just beginning to enjoy our daily heated discussions, when one day he refused to engage any further. "I can't argue with you anymore," he said. "But I want you to read this."

He handed me a letter, which I read on the bus ride home. In it, he spelled out the Gospel and said that he would be praying for my salvation. We didn't talk much after that, and I stopped thinking about the conflict between evolution and the Bible. But the Gospel continued to lurk in the back of my mind.

It wasn't until I graduated from high school that it resurfaced; and this time, I was the one who sought it out. I had a growing desire to find a purpose in life, and it occurred to me that if there *were* in fact an all-powerful, loving God, it would be stupid not to pursue him. Plus, my twentieth birthday was looming closely in the future. I would need to decide soon what I was going to do about that vow to become a minister.

And so I began seeking.

The most obvious place to start was my own Bible. I had a red-letter edition—with all of the words spoken by Christ printed in red ink—that I had been given by my church when I entered third grade. I took it down from my shelf, peeled the gilt-edged pages apart, and turned to the Gospel of Matthew, determined to read everything written in red. I would judge Jesus' teachings for myself.

I began with the Sermon on the Mount and read all the way through to the Lord's Prayer, where I stopped to reflect. For some reason, I was stunned by what Jesus said about prayer, that we should pray in secret and not use many words—*for your Father knows what you need before you ask him.* This, to me, was fresh teaching. I had been going to church my whole life, but I felt as if I had never heard this message before.

Right there at my desk, I decided that the church I'd been

attending for so many years wasn't following Jesus' teaching at all. Why did we have all those lengthy prayers during the service? Was that not direct disobedience of a command—or if not a command, at least a clear instruction—from Christ himself?

In those few pages, I saw for the first time the revolutionary nature of Jesus' words, the enormous leap that he had made to a new, more enlightened morality. It wasn't just wrong to murder someone, he said, but to *desire* to harm someone. And it was wrong to judge people. In a single sermon, Jesus had demolished legalism and hypocrisy. Being a good person wasn't about just refraining from hurting others. You had to be good on the inside. You had to rid yourself of hatred and the desire to do wrong.

Jesus was calling for us to be perfect. It was an impossible standard, of course—hence the need for grace. We fall short of the perfection required for us to have fellowship with a holy God, but by putting our faith in Christ, we throw our lot in with him; and since he is perfect, communion with God becomes possible. This was the idea that I had been failing to grasp during all those years of attending church, Sunday school, and youth group. *This* was the Gospel.

Immediately, I wanted to share my newfound understanding. Even before closing my Bible, I was fantasizing about founding a church based solely on the Sermon on the Mount. Surely, I thought, these words were inspired by God. Had I read other passages—such as those in which God orders the Israelites to commit genocide—I might have drawn a more tempered conclusion. But all I saw at that moment was pure wisdom.

I called my friend Joseph, another classmate who was a born-again Christian, and told him of the revelations I had just had about Jesus. Having decided that Jesus was divine, I wanted to know how I could be born again, too. And Joseph told me that it was simple. All I needed to do was pray—to confess to God that I was a sinner and invite Jesus into my heart. After explaining this, Joseph offered to pray with me over the phone, and I accepted.

His prayer went on for quite some time, but despite having just read Jesus' exhortation to keep our prayers short, it didn't bother me. I was intoxicated. Joseph prayed that God would show me how much he loved me and that I would receive Christ as my savior. I echoed his words in my own mind, begging God to reveal himself and to save me. When he had finished praying, Joseph told me to keep reading my Bible and to stay in touch with him. Then we hung up.

For several minutes, I sat there processing our conversation. And then I began to feel it: the most intense exhilaration I'd ever experienced. Like a drug with a delayed effect, it had now had time to course through my veins and saturate my body. I got up and looked at myself in the mirror. *God loves me*, I thought. Suddenly, I couldn't stop smiling. Joseph had prayed that God would show me how much he loved me, and God was now granting that request. But more importantly, I had confessed my sins and accepted Christ as my savior.

I had been born again.

2

Transformed by the Spirit

An unnatural silence descended upon the room, and I felt my face turning red as it became the focus of seven pairs of momentarily-widened eyes. A newly-matriculated physics major at Rice University, I was sitting in a Bible study sponsored by Campus Crusade for Christ—and I had just declared that I didn't believe in hell.

In a coincidence that was clearly part of God's plan to help me grow in my new faith, it had turned out that my roommate, Eric, was also a born-again Christian. Through him, I had met other believers and found this Bible study. And I was just now beginning to realize that I didn't quite fit the evangelical mold. True, I had been born again; but I had some transformations to undergo yet.

I'm not sure how I expected the others to respond to my declaration. Somewhere in the back of my mind, I must have imagined that they would all chime in, saying, "Yeah, there's no way a loving God would send people to hell." But that's not what happened. All they did was stare in shock. And then the Bible study leader, Patrick, emitted an awkward chuckle. Behind his smile, he seemed to be thinking, "He'll come around."

And I did.

I came around in other ways, too. Ever since studying evolution back in ninth grade, I had believed that humans had descended from a self-replicating molecule that formed in a primordial soup billions of years ago. And during my first months as a born-again Christian, I saw no contradictions between the Bible and evolution. In particular, I assumed that the creation story in Genesis was intended to be interpreted metaphorically.

But soon I was bombarded with arguments that evolution was not just wrong but a diabolical lie. It denied humans the dignity of being specially created in the image of God, and it undermined the Gospel. At many Christian friends' urging, I began reading books by apologists who aimed to show that creationism was more reasonable than evolution. Before long, I convinced myself that evolution might not be true after all.

My sense of morality changed as well. Whereas I had once been a liberal relativist, I soon became a conservative absolutist—particularly with regard to sex. Things that previously wouldn't have bothered me now petrified me with horror. I was aghast one night when I heard the sounds of an orgasm coming through the wall of a neighboring dorm room. And when the Christian community mounted a campaign against Rice's annual "Night of Decadence"—a beer-soaked orgy of a costume party—I jumped on board.

Then there was the issue of language. Ever since middle school, I had been in the habit of seasoning my speech with expletives. Nearly every other word out of my mouth—when there were no adults present—was "fuck" or "shit." It did not occur to me that this was something I should change upon becoming a Christian. But one day, Eric confided to me that a friend had asked him, "Are you sure your roommate's a Christian? He curses like a sailor."

Eric had responded by telling his friend that I attended a Bible study and called myself a Christian, so he supposed I was. I felt grateful that he had vouched for me, but I was alarmed that someone had doubted my faith because of my language. I asked Eric what exactly was wrong with cursing, and he explained that the problem wasn't so much the words themselves as the inner attitude that they belied. If you stub your toe, yelling "shit" reveals a spirit of anger that you should aspire to purge.

One could do so, he said, incrementally. First, you might start by making an effort to say "shoot" instead of "shit" whenever you stub your toe. After you master that, you can shift your focus to remaining *calm* when you say "shoot." Then you can resist saying anything at all—Eric illustrated by pounding once on his chest in lieu of cursing—and finally, you reach a point where you don't even feel an *impulse* to cry out. If you stub your toe, you just keep going without experiencing any anger.

The strategy didn't sound promising to me, but I decided to try it—with one slight modification. The word I chose to substitute for all expletives—and I'm not really sure why—was "penis." For months, in every situation where I normally would have said "shit" or "fuck," I said "penis" instead. This resulted in all sorts of absurd ejaculations, including, "What the penis?" and "Holy penile insurrection."

Hearing these words come out of my own mouth had a comic effect that immediately dulled the edge of my anger. The more absurd the phrase, the stronger the effect. And it wasn't long before—as Eric had said—the urge to say anything at all had vanished, and I stopped shouting about penises. After a year, my temper had melted away entirely, and I was more tranquil than I'd ever been.

There were other contributing factors to my transformation, of course. I spent an hour every day praying and reading scripture. My belief that God loved me gave me a deeply satisfying sense of purpose. I knew that I would be spending eternity in heaven, and God was with me wherever I went. On one occasion, a classmate asked me, with some annoyance, "How can you always be so cheerful?"

"Because God is so good to me," I said.

My newfound peace prevailed even under extreme circumstances. On the day before Thanksgiving, my left lung spontaneously collapsed. I was rushed to the hospital for surgery, and for two weeks I had a tube protruding from my chest, running to a pump that kept my lung inflated. I was in constant pain and didn't relish having Thanksgiving dinner in the hospital, but I felt a deep sense of joy throughout it all.

On another occasion, I was rear-ended by a distracted driver while waiting for a fire truck to cross in front of me at an intersection. The other driver's wrist had been broken in the impact, but I emerged unscathed. Nevertheless, the paramedics suggested that I go to the hospital to get checked out, and they loaded me into the ambulance together with the woman who had hit me. During the ride, I asked about her family and prayed that her wrist would heal quickly.

The paramedics were astonished. "I've never seen anything like this before," one of them told my father. "Usually when we have the two parties of a car accident in the same ambulance, we can't get them to stop screaming at each other."

That peace was, I thought, evidence of the Holy Spirit. So too was the feeling that rushed over me whenever I sang praise songs in a group. At least once a semester, the Christian ministries at Rice would organize a praise-and-worship concert. They were like drugs to me. All around me, people were crying, lifting their hands, and dancing. I thought that nothing but the Holy Spirit could account for the exhilaration I felt during those events. And so it surprised me when, at a Christian retreat, I was told that I was *still* missing something.

At lunch, a guy named Andrés sat beside me and said that I was only experiencing half of the life that God intended for me. The other half would come with baptism by the Holy

Spirit, he said; speaking in tongues would liberate me. He picked up my Bible—which I always had on me—and opened it to the book of Acts. He showed me some verses about the Holy Spirit—verses about glossolalia, prophecy, healing, and even teleportation. These were things that *all* believers were supposed to experience.

Andrés gave me a pamphlet that he had written about how baptism by the Holy Spirit had rescued him from the clutches of pornography and masturbation, and he told me that there would be a meeting that evening for those who wanted to receive the Holy Spirit. Although it wasn't an official part of the retreat, a lot of people would be there.

I was interested, but when Andrés got up and left the table, the leader of our campus ministry, Darin, took his place. "We don't approve of what he's teaching people," Darin said. "It would really be a bad idea for you to get involved with him."

I didn't understand Darin's objection. After all, Andrés was only teaching what was written in the Bible. But the admonition was enough to stop me from going to that meeting. Nevertheless, everything that Andrés had said stayed with me. The power offered by the Holy Spirit sounded wonderful, and I hoped that I would receive it one day.

In the meantime, nothing was more important than sharing the Gospel. The fate of the souls of everyone around me was, quite literally, a cosmic emergency of incomparable magnitude. There was simply no excuse for sitting next to someone—in class, on a bus, or on a plane—and *not* sharing the

Gospel with them. In fact, that was our main purpose in life.

There was nothing irrational about this way of thinking. It was the only conclusion that could be drawn from the axioms of my faith. If the Christian god was real, if heaven and hell were real, and if the only way to avoid hell was to receive Christ as one's savior, then there was absolutely no morally acceptable course of action except to devote oneself wholeheartedly to sharing the Gospel.

Whenever I felt hesitant or embarrassed to proclaim my faith—which was quite often—I pushed myself all the harder to do so. I wrote letters to my friends, telling them how Christ had transformed me and exhorting them to surrender to Jesus. I even wrote a letter to the executive who was in charge of renewing my National Merit Scholarship each year, telling him that I had been saved.

Despite my discomfort in sharing the Gospel, I was content with my new life; and the transformations I had undergone relieved me of a burden that had been plaguing me for years. I was not just convinced that God existed, but I was utterly devoted to him; and as a result, I was finally in a position to fulfill the vow that I had made as a terrified little boy so long ago. At last, I could become a minister in good conscience.

Still, there was one little thing that nagged me.

I had always been an inquisitive person by nature, and I loved contemplating philosophical and scientific mysteries with an open mind. But as I delved more deeply into Christianity, certain questions were no longer open to honest inquiry:

Could the authors of the gospels have distorted historical facts? Had humans evolved from other species? Was our universe the product of a giant explosion?

To a fundamentalist Christian—which I now called myself—such questions were only fair game if approached with an *a priori* understanding that the answers must support certain foregone conclusions—namely, that the Bible was the inerrant word of God and that both the universe and humanity were designed and created by him. From this perspective, every intellectual inquiry ultimately turned into a puzzle that could be summarized in a simple question: How can I harmonize my observations with the core beliefs that I am unwilling to abandon?

For the most part, I enjoyed tackling such puzzles; but deep down, I knew that the approach was inherently disingenuous. An honest inquiry ought to be undertaken with the humble acknowledgement that any belief, no matter how cherished it is, might turn out to be wrong. In the presence of steadfast faith, however, such genuine inquiry was no longer possible. And so as a result of my newfound relationship with God, I had given up the luxury of free thought.

3

Einstein, Jesus, and a Girl Named Nellie

The email came out of nowhere, and I wasn't sure how to respond. It was from Clay—the first person who had ever shared the Gospel with me, the first person I'd ever heard say, "I don't believe in evolution." We hadn't talked in years; and suddenly he was writing to me not about Jesus, but something else entirely.

Clay had recently become interested in physics; and having heard that I was a physics major, he wanted to connect with me over his new passion. His dream was to understand the very fabric of existence. "I'm particularly fascinated," he wrote, "by John Wheeler's concept of 'it from bit'." He was referring to the most recent revolution in physics: the idea that reality, at its most fundamental level, consisted of *information* rather than spacetime and matter.

Everything Clay wrote resonated with me. I, too, longed to understand the Big Bang, the fourteen-billion-year history of our universe, and the nature of spacetime. I dreamed of tackling the problem of quantum gravity, which had frustrated Einstein himself until the day he died, and I wanted to know whether we were made of superstrings, quantum loops, or something yet unimagined. Every month or so, I would walk into Barnes and Noble just to heft and stroke their lone copy of John Wheeler's *Gravitation* while fantasizing about mastering cosmology (which is not the study of cosmetics, as one of my roommates kept insisting, but the study of the *cosmos*—the word physicists use to refer to all of existence).

I was overjoyed that Clay had reached out to me. Now we could connect not just over our zeal for physics, but our love of Christ. Surely this was a beautiful part of God's plan, to reunite me with the person who had first shared the Gospel with me and to give us common interests.

In my reply, I hardly mentioned physics at all. Instead, I reminded Clay of our conversation back in ninth grade about sin and redemption, and of the letter he had written to me saying that he would pray for me. I wrote that I was now saved, thanks in large part to his courage, and that I longed to commune with him.

He never wrote back.

After some time, I began to wonder whether he was still a believer. Had he been unable to reconcile his former evangelical faith with his newfound understanding of science?

The question caused me to reflect on my own attempts to reconcile the two. I was certain that they *were* reconcilable, and I was intensely interested in constructing a rational basis for believing in the resurrection of Christ, the historical accuracy of the Bible, and the literal account of creation as recorded in Genesis. To this end, I had begun devouring all available literature on evangelical apologetics.

Faith was crucial, of course; but God was a rational being who had created us with tools of reason in order that we might know him better. We glorified God when we used those tools in his service. By means of reason, I believed that I could harmonize my love of science with my faith in the Word of God.

It was, in retrospect, a severe case of cognitive dissonance: My mind was ensconced in an unstable superposition of orthogonal states. That in itself was enough to make a mess out of me. But then, to top it all off, I fell in love.

It was the spring semester of my junior year, and I had developed a crush on a fifth-year student named Nellie. She was an athletic Chinese-American girl from Garland, Texas, who had a petite frame, large round eyes, and an ebullient spirit. She was pretty, she was popular, and she loved God with all of her heart—in short, she was everything a young evangelical guy like me could ever hope for.

There was a potential problem, however. Nellie had been dating another guy, an equally hardcore Christian named Mark, for years. Supposedly, they had broken up; but they still appeared to be good friends—such good friends, in fact, that most people thought they were still dating. There was a general consensus in our community that Nellie and Mark were made for each other, and that fate—or rather, the will of God—would bring them back together sooner or later.

Wanting neither to embarrass myself nor to make an enemy of a brother in Christ, I decided to consult with Mark before I made any moves. And so one day, I sat down with him in my dorm room after we'd just finished throwing a Frisbee around, and I asked him point-blank whether he was still interested in Nellie.

"No way, man," he said. "There's no way I'll ever get back together with her. You have my blessing."

He couldn't have spoken more clearly or more firmly. It didn't occur to me that his adamancy might be an indicator that Nellie had some quirks that would make a romantic relationship with her difficult. My only care at the moment was that she was free; Mark would not be a rival.

And so I made my interest known. I invited Nellie to a school dance; I took her out to dinner; I went jogging with her. Once, when I was giving her a ride, I shared with her that I had recently developed an allergy to my favorite brand of deodorant; and she reciprocated by telling me about two newlyweds who had met another couple at a hotel, invited them back to their room for drinks, and murdered them for the fun of it. Her morbid fascination with the story disturbed me, but I decided not to worry about it.

Nellie consented to go out with me on numerous occasions, and we spent quite a bit of time together. Nevertheless, she didn't seem that interested in me. In fact, she said outright that she just wanted to be friends. I wasn't about to let that deter me, though. I was prepared to exercise biblical persistence. I could be Jacob, and she would be my Rachel.

Meanwhile, the time was fast approaching for me to decide what I would do during the coming summer. The previous year, I had worked in a physics lab, where I built circuits for a system of lasers that would cool clouds of strontium atoms almost down to absolute zero so that their wave-like behavior could be observed. This year, I wanted to go on a mission trip with Campus Crusade for Christ—or "Cru," as we were just beginning to call it. The leaders of Cru were planning trips to three destinations, and I agonized over which one was right for me.

Nellie was at the forefront of my mind as I mulled over the choices. Like many people in our circle of friends, she too was interested in missions. She had been on several summer trips, including more than one to East Asia; and to her, such trips were small potatoes. She planned to go into long-term ministry, and she wanted to do it in China. In fact, she was going to spend the following year there—and quite possibly the rest of her life. Naturally, I took this into account when thinking about where I would go for the summer. My options were Florida, China, and Mexico.

I chose Mexico.

A summer in Florida sounded more like a vacation than a mission trip to me. To a lot of people, that would have been a strong reason to go there. But the way I saw things, it just wasn't a place for serious missionaries who harbored romantic notions about suffering for Christ in exotic and impoverished locales. The gate to heaven was supposed to be narrow, and the path difficult. But if ever there was a smooth path through a wide gate, it was the one through Panama City Beach, Florida. And so in my mind, Florida was never a legitimate option.

China, on the other hand—or rather, East Asia—was the ultimate destination in missions. It was, as I understood it, a poor, atheist nation that was run somewhat like a concentration camp by the communist party. It harbored over a billion unreached souls. Life there promised to be uncomfortable, fraught with culture shock, language barriers, and bowel ailments. To a hardcore Christian—which is what I aspired to be—these qualities made China the place to go, and it was easily my first choice.

As I thought about going to China, however, I was plagued by two thoughts. One was about my brother. He had been on mission trips to Russia and Korea, which were exotic places in my mind. Part of me thought that if I chose China, I might be doing so only as a way to compete with him. More important, though, was Nellie. If I went to China, would I be going there just to impress her? This question really nagged at me. I wanted to be sure that my heart was pure; and it seemed that Mexico was the only place that allowed me no ulterior motives.

There were other reasons this decision made sense. I had studied Spanish in high school, and I had been to Mexico several times for short-term trips—Gospel-bombing missions in which we would drop in at a university campus, share the Gospel with everyone in sight for a few days, and go back to America, most likely never again to contact the people we thought we had saved. With that experience, I would surely be more productive in Mexico than in China.

There were a lot of preparations to be made. The trip would cost about three thousand dollars—enough to cover transportation, food, housing, and tuition for Spanish courses at Monterrey Tec. To raise the money, I wrote letters to friends, family, and fellow church members asking for support.

In the meantime, Nellie was mounting her own campaign to raise over $30,000 for her upcoming year in China. To no one's surprise, so also was Mark. Since they were petitioning many of the same donors—mostly wealthy people at our church—they would be driving around a lot together. If not for that conversation I'd had with Mark, I might have felt threatened. But his words had been clear and final, and I was confident that Nellie would remain free for me to pursue.

Just before I was to leave for Mexico, Mark called me. "I need to talk to you," he said. "Can you meet me for lunch?"

We met at a barbecue restaurant near our church. After getting our food at the buffet, we found a table and sat down. Then, with visible reluctance, Mark said what was on his mind.

"Nellie and I are getting back together."

My chopped brisket sandwich turned to ashes in my mouth. I stared at him for a moment, wondering how I was supposed to respond. Should I leap across the table and grab his throat? Get up and storm out of the restaurant? No. I could be as meek as Jesus wanted me to be.

All I did was nod.

"I'm sorry," Mark said. "It just kind of happened."

In the following days, I told myself that this was an opportunity to show God how faithful I could be. Nellie had been an idol to me, and even after choosing Mexico over China, I had continued clinging to her. Now I had to let go in truth. It was time for me to focus single-mindedly on spreading the Gospel, with no fleshly distractions.

It turned out that Mexico wasn't bad.

During my two months there, I haunted the campus of Monterrey Tec, pestering students with Gospel tracts and invitations to join a Bible study. I discovered the wonders of *horchata*, a beverage imported directly from heaven. And at a grimy wooden shack on a dusty road near my dorm, I consumed the most succulent avocado cheeseburger the world has ever known. Also, compulsively, I weighed and measured every girl I met—but each time, all I could think was, "She's not Nellie."

Before I knew it, I was back in Houston, getting ready for my fourth year of college. Nellie and Mark, who had spent every evening of the summer soliciting donations and doing God knows what else in Mark's car, were wrapping up their fundraising campaign and preparing to leave for East Asia. They would be in separate cities, but from my point of view, they were as hitched as two people could be. The best thing I could do would be to forget about Nellie.

That fall, I buried myself in my studies. In keeping with my cosmological aspirations, I took courses in particle physics, topology, and non-Euclidean geometry. And in seeking to strengthen my faith, I spent my free time reading the apologetic works of Lee Strobel, Josh McDowell, and Michael Behe. I took comfort in the thought that the earliest martyrs would only have died willingly if they had truly witnessed the resurrected Christ; and I pumped my fist when I read about examples of irreducibly complex biological systems that could not possibly have evolved under natural forces alone.

I remained highly involved in Cru, playing drums at our worship meetings and leading a weekly men's Bible study. And as always, I stayed on the lookout for mission opportunities. I was finally beginning to move past my infatuation with Nellie, and I figured that I could now go to China without fear of being governed by impure motives. I was therefore thrilled when Cru announced plans for a week-long trip to East Asia over Christmas break.

The destination was the city where Mark was living, and the objective was to aid him in his evangelistic work. Most likely, Nellie would even come visit the team during the trip. If I went, not only would I have to work with Mark, but I would see him and Nellie together. It was therefore bound to be a painful experience for me.

I signed up immediately.

4

Spies for Christ

Our mission was to drop the "Four Boys"—the Gospel, in the form of the "Four Spiritual Laws"—on college students. Since proselytizing was illegal in China, we would have to go in like spies. And so a week before our departure, our little team of four was given a "security briefing."

The first order of business was to disguise our Bibles. Stella, a Cru staffer who had been to China before, showed us the proper method. It was exactly how I had covered my textbooks in elementary school: with a cut-up brown paper grocery bag.

To me, the precaution seemed futile, if not counterproductive—wouldn't a covered book draw more suspicion than an uncovered one? I imagined communist Chinese officers walking down the aisle of our plane, searching our luggage for Christian paraphernalia. Surely they would find the covered book in my possession, and, upon opening it, recognize it for what it was. Who could say what would happen then?

But that was the protocol.

The second order of business was to learn the code words used by Cru's missionaries. Instead of "China," we were to say "East Asia," which we already knew because so many of our friends had gone before us. The other words were new to me, though. Instead of identifying someone as "Christian," we would say they were "Cool," and a Bible was to be referred to only as a "Text."

Most important of all, to protect our organization, we had to call it "The Company." I later learned that this had been a code word for the CIA during the Cold War; and in retrospect, it seems positively stupid for a missionary organization to adopt a word with such a history. I suppose this was precisely what gave it its allure, though; it was exciting to think of ourselves as secret agents.

Not wanting to be an ill-prepared secret agent, I asked several experienced missionaries what life as a Christian was like in China. They told me that there were above-ground churches, but they were controlled by the government. Their meetings were monitored, and sermons were screened by Party officials. The books of Genesis, Romans, and Revelation were banned, and the names of all church attendees and Bible purchasers were documented. People caught attending an underground church, sharing the Gospel, or possessing

Christian literature were often imprisoned, beaten, and forced to renounce their faith.

Under these circumstances, it was clear that we had a moral imperative to slip into the country and aid the oppressed masses of underground believers. Doing so would be dangerous; but what could be nobler or more exhilarating than risking life and limb for Christ?

On the morning of our flight, we gathered before sunrise. Groggy but excited, we drove to the airport, made our way through security, and boarded our plane. We had a layover in Los Angeles and then another in Tokyo, where my American ego suffered its first blow. The bathrooms there were high-tech and sparkling-clean—like nothing I had ever seen. *How can this be?* I thought. *Doesn't America lead the world in technology?*

After one more flight, we touched down in Shanghai, deep in communist territory, and as the plane pulled up to the gate, I stretched my legs, trying to recall the symptoms of deep vein thrombosis. At that moment, Amy—one of the Cru staffers—was overcome by excitement that the flight had ended at last and said in a loud voice, "Praise the Lord!"

I turned to look at her, and her eyes widened. Nervously, she glanced around, hoping that no one had heard the religious exclamation. She appeared to be expecting a SWAT team to burst in through the airplane windows and whisk her away to an underground torture chamber. Nothing happened, though, and we got off the plane and went through customs.

Mark was there to meet us. He ushered us out of the

airport and past a swarm of unlicensed taxi drivers who were clamoring for our attention. We stopped at a pair of tiny "bread loaf" vans, and Mark spoke to the drivers in Chinese. They would take us to our final destination: a city that we were to name under no circumstances.

The ride took three hours. I sat crushed between a pile of luggage on my left and Patrick, my former Bible study leader, on my right. There wasn't enough room for my knees, so I had to pull my legs up and twist to the side just to fit. I wanted nothing more than to sleep, but I just wasn't able.

Mark played tour guide, but I was too uncomfortable to pay attention. The mad swerving as our driver tried to pass every car on the road was beginning to make me feel both ill and sore. The van seemed to have no shock absorbers, and my seat was little more than a wooden plank bolted to the frame.

At that moment, I hated myself.

We had only just arrived, and I already felt stretched beyond my tolerance for discomfort—which had turned out to be embarrassingly low. I was upset that the ride was so unpleasant, and I was ashamed that I couldn't handle it. Secretly, I hoped that the others were as uncomfortable as I was and that they too were barely managing not to complain.

At last, we arrived at a hotel, and Mark helped us check in. It turned out that I would be rooming with Patrick. Mark escorted us to our room, and when we entered it, I had never been so happy to see a bed before. There was a sign on the wall above it that said, "Please don't burn in bed."

No problem, I thought as I dove onto the mattress. But it

wasn't a mattress. It was a thin layer of foam on top of a solid wooden platform. There was a loud crunch when I landed, and my hip exploded in pain. Mark and Patrick turned to look at me when they heard the sound, concern battling amusement on their faces.

As I nursed my bruised hip, Mark turned on the TV at maximum volume and started chatting with us. It didn't make sense to me to have the volume so high if we were going to talk, so I reached over and turned it down. But Mark shook his head and turned it back up. He explained that this way, if the room was bugged, the listeners wouldn't be able to make out what we were saying.

After a while, we prayed, and Mark left.

The next morning, Mark arrived with another long-term missionary named Kirk to help us find breakfast. We made our way down the hill atop which our hotel was perched and came to a major intersection, where a street vendor stood on the corner.

I examined my meal when it was handed to me, and Mark explained what it was. It was the most typical thing you can find in China, something called a *youtiao*, which literally means "oil stick." It's basically a deep-fried length of dough, over a foot long, and it's usually folded and wrapped in a big egg tortilla with some minced vegetables, soy sauce, and spicy peppers.

With our meals in hand, we set off for the head missionary's house, chewing and chatting as we walked. The *youtiao* was as oily as its name implied, and salty besides, but otherwise quite good. When I had finished off the last bite and was licking the juice from my fingers, Kirk began recounting an interesting story about *youtiao*.

He said that just the previous year, one of the vendors had tried to get an edge on his competitors by putting rat poison in their flour supplies. The guy had only intended for people to feel ill after eating their *youtiao*; but he failed to conduct adequate research on rat poison dosages before carrying out the stunt, and several people died.

"Did they catch the guy?" I asked.

"Yep," Kirk replied.

"What did they do to him?"

"Put a bullet in his head." Kirk made a gun shape with his hand and fired it. "Chinese justice is swift," he added.

I stared back at him, wide-eyed, wondering whether it was too late to induce vomiting. I guess Kirk could read my expression, because he explained, "Don't worry. It's safer now than it ever was. No one's going to try *that* again."

After a bit more walking, we arrived at the home of the head missionary, a guy named Tom. He had a wife and two kids, and he taught English at one of the local universities. We convened in his living room, and when we finished introducing ourselves, Tom explained what we would be doing. It was simple: We would share the Gospel with students at the universities where the long-term missionaries studied Chinese or taught English.

After hearing Mark talk about the possibility of our hotel rooms being bugged, I had become quite conscious of security.

But here, Tom was talking openly about sharing the Gospel with Chinese students. I asked him whether it was really safe to talk freely in his apartment, and in response, he looked up at the smoke detector—which would have been an obvious place to plant a bug—and spoke to it.

"That was Henry Rambow, from Rice University!"

Without bothering to explain how he could be sure that his apartment wasn't bugged, Tom went on to say that since we would only be in the country for a week, there was no risk to us if we shared the Gospel openly. If caught, we would simply not be allowed to come back to China in the future. The long-term missionaries, on the other hand, had a lot more to worry about. They wanted to protect their ties to the schools and remain in the country. Consequently, they had to be more discreet about what they shared with the locals.

The most important part of our job was to gauge the students' response to the Gospel and then tell the long-term missionaries which ones seemed interested. They could then follow up by inviting the students to Bible studies and connecting them to house churches. When Tom finished explaining all of this, it was time for us to begin our mission, and we took a taxi to one of the schools.

The campus was the physical embodiment of communism. The architecture was stark. Every building was gray and square, and the layout was perfectly symmetrical. The view was dominated by a statue of Chairman Mao, his head held high and his hand outstretched to salute the people. Even the hallways inside the buildings had bare concrete floors and stark plaster walls. If ever a place was in need of the light of Christ, this was it.

We began in Kirk's English class. We introduced ourselves to everybody, and then each of us was teamed up with two or three students of our own gender—the last thing we wanted was to complicate our mission with hormones—with whom we walked around the campus and chatted. As far as the university knew, that was why we were there—to help their students learn English.

The two students I was with introduced themselves as David and Andy. They took me to the one part of the campus that didn't have that stark, blocky feel. It was a garden with a path that wound around some manmade hills. There were plants, but since it was the heart of winter, everything looked dead, adding to the bleakness. We stopped at a pagoda and sat down to talk.

"Can you sing a song for us?" David asked.

Seeing an opportunity to steer our conversation to the Gospel, I sang the first verse of "Amazing Grace" and explained the meaning of the lyrics. David and Andy were pleased, and they reciprocated by singing a traditional Chinese song, which I of course didn't recognize. Then they asked how much Chinese I knew.

Years before, when I was in middle school, a friend had taught me a few sentences, including "Go hit him," and "Go kill him." We had amused ourselves by saying these things to his three-year-old cousin, and I still remembered the words. But now, with Andy and David looking at me expectantly, I decided not to bring that up. Instead, I told them that I spoke none at all.

"Repeat after me," Andy said. He cleared his throat, held up one finger, and said, "Eeee!"

"Eeee!" I repeated.

Then he held up two fingers, and I realized that he was teaching me how to count. "Err!" he shouted.

Before I could repeat the word for two, David interrupted. "No, it's more like 'are'," he said.

For the next few minutes, the two of them argued like characters in a Monty Python sketch about the pronunciation of the word for "two." I waited patiently, wondering whether I would ever make it to three, until at last David said, "Don't listen to Andy. He's from the countryside and speaks with an accent."

David completed my lesson on the numbers one through ten, and then he and Andy quizzed me for a while to make sure I had retained everything. When they were satisfied with my progress, we left the pagoda and returned to the classroom just in time for the bell to ring.

In the next class, I was grouped with three guys who decided to take me to their dorm room, which was tiny and smelled of feces. They ushered me into a chair and gathered around me to talk. As before, I was waiting for an opportunity to tell them about God; and just when I was thinking about how to bring him up, one student said, "I have a question."

"Go ahead," I said.

"In America, you have something written on your money:

'In God We Trust.' What does that mean?"

There couldn't have been a wider opening for me to drop the Four Boys. I took a dollar bill out of my wallet, pointed to it as I spoke, and explained what it meant to trust in God. I also tried to make it clear that, although the money was printed by the government, Americans were not required to believe in God.

I wrapped up my explanation, and we all sat for a moment staring at the dollar bill in my hand. Then I thought, "Hey, what better way to ensure that they remember my explanation than to give them a dollar bill?" So I removed two more bills from my wallet and handed one to each of the students, not realizing the effect it would have. Feeling obligated to reciprocate, they insisted on giving me Chinese bills of greater value.

When we left their room, they showed me around the rest of the building, proudly introducing me to their friends and inviting others to join us. Soon there were about eight guys gathered around me as we walked the hallways of the building. And then it happened again: Without any prompting, one of the newcomers gave me the sort of opportunity that I was waiting for.

"Do you have words of hope?" he asked.

"What do you mean?" I said.

"Can you tell me about Jesus Christ?" he asked.

I gaped. And then I proceeded to share the Gospel, standing in the small crowd just as I imagined Christ had stood among his followers when delivering the Sermon on the

Mount. The fact that not just one, but two students had asked me to tell them about God indicated that these students were beyond hungry for the Gospel; they were starving.

When it was time to go for a walk with my third group of students, I was feeling emboldened. Since people in the previous two groups had asked me directly about God, there seemed to be nothing to worry about. So this time, without any prompting at all, I asked, "Do you believe in God?"

One of the students looked at me with narrowed eyes and said, "*God* is a bad word here. Let's talk about something else." I blinked and then made the quiet decision to keep the Four Boys to myself this time. Not everyone, it seemed, was starved for words of hope.

5

A Sword and a Stalker

It didn't take long to find a place that sold weapons. The stall was just like all the others in the market, but it had swords, spears, and daggers hanging on the back wall. Behind the counter, an elderly couple sat on stools, watching the passing tourists with beady eyes, likely searching for young men like me—their most reliable prey.

As soon as the old man caught sight of me, he leapt from his stool and began taking items down at random for me to examine. I shook my head and pointed behind him at the piece that had caught my eye: a sword in a darkly stained wooden scabbard.

He handed it to me, and I tried to unsheathe it to see what the blade looked like. But it wouldn't budge. I was just beginning to think that it was fake—a hilt glued to the end of a scabbard—when the old man took it from my hands and yanked it free with a fierce jerk. The blade was shiny, with a mirror finish, and it had carvings of dragons near the hilt.

It was perfect.

Over the past few days, my team and I had established the pattern of proselytizing during the day and touring the city at night. At the moment, we were engaged in the latter activity in a popular souvenir market. The girls in our group had run off in search of pirated DVDs, while I—having cast a disapproving frown upon them—had set off with Mark on a far more legitimate quest: to procure a sword.

Now, as Mark and I looked on, the wizened old vendor held the blade out before us and shook it with a vigorous flourish. It wobbled, and he turned to us with a pleased expression on his face. Clearly, he was quite proud of the quality of his ware.

I wasn't sure, however, that a sword was *supposed* to wobble. Was the man proud that it *was* wobbly, or that it had wobbled so little? I would have asked Mark, but I felt too embarrassed to admit ignorance on what was evidently a critical criterion for judging the quality of a blade. So I just smiled and nodded to indicate that I was impressed.

"How much?" I asked.

As if by magic, the old man's wife appeared by his side and handed him a calculator. He punched some numbers on it and showed me the display: two hundred kuai. That converted to about twenty-four dollars. It wasn't too bad, really, but I knew that I was supposed to bargain.

"That's too expensive," I said.

The man didn't say a word. Instead, he handed me the calculator, gesturing for me to enter my own number. I hesitated, typed in one hundred and fifty, and started to hand it back. But Mark stopped me with a surreptitious nudge.

"You can get it for a hundred," he said.

The words had barely left Mark's mouth when the old man exploded. Mark took a step back, and I watched, my adrenaline suddenly flowing, as the man scolded him in Chinese. When the barrage was over, I looked questioningly at Mark.

"He's angry that I'm helping you," Mark said.

I looked back at the old man. He had a sour expression on his face that mirrored my own feelings. After his little tirade, I no longer felt comfortable, and I just wanted to finish bargaining as soon as possible. I figured that the best way to proceed would be to offer a hundred kuai and then accept his counter offer, regardless of what it was.

"One hundred," I said.

Roars of derisive laughter erupted from the old man and his wife, and they shoved crooked index fingers in my face. I was so shocked and offended that I turned to walk away, not caring to wait for a counter offer. Immediately, the elderly couple's contemptuous smiles evaporated, and they began tripping over each other to shout "Okay!"

I paused for a minute.

I thought about saying no—I didn't want to do any

business with them at all after hearing that laugh—but I realized that if I still wanted a sword, I would have to start the process over somewhere else. So I handed over a hundred kuai and left with the sword, grudgingly thankful for Mark's help.

The next day, after a morning filled with more proselytizing, I went with Mark to his apartment. Despite the situation with Nellie, we were still friends, and we had some catching up to do. He showed me around, and I commented on how tiny the place was—not to insult him, but to convey my respect for his ability to sacrifice his comfort.

"You have no idea," he said. "To most of the students here, this is a palace. I feel embarrassed to have my Chinese friends over, because they all think I'm rich."

Palace or not, his apartment was cramped, and we decided to go for a walk around the neighborhood. We were chatting, trying to avoid any mention of Nellie, when we rounded a corner, and there before us were two hulking soldiers in uniform ambling along with their backs to us. If we kept going at our current pace, we would pass them.

My first inclination was to keep walking and ignore them. Anything else might only draw attention. But Mark grabbed my elbow, pulled me back around the corner, and took me another way. The move seemed rather extreme. Wasn't he being overly cautious? Could life for a Christian in China really be so dangerous?

I chewed on these questions until it was time for dinner. Mark and I met the rest of the team at a restaurant, and I saw that another person had joined them: Nellie. The moment that I had been dreading had arrived at last. I was going to have to spend an evening watching Mark and Nellie together.

Nothing about the meal went as I had imagined it would go. There was no hand-holding, and there were no fawning looks into each other's eyes. In fact, they didn't sit together at all—or even talk to teach other. It was downright infuriating how flagrantly discreet they were being. And it was ironic: Back when they had only been friends, they had always looked like they were dating. But now that they were dating, they didn't even look like friends.

I tried to think on other things, but each time Nellie laughed, my old feelings for her bubbled up, and I ended up spending the entirety of the meal trying to hide my attraction. I was just thinking that I was succeeding, when Mark touched my arm. I turned and saw in his eyes an expression that said we needed to talk privately about something.

I leaned toward him, expecting him to tell me to back off, and he raised his hand to point. But instead of pointing at Nellie or me, he directed my gaze across the restaurant.

"That guy's been watching us for a long time," he said.

The man Mark was talking about sat alone on the other side of the room. Wearing a suit with no tie, he looked to be in his thirties. He was holding a newspaper, but he kept glancing up to look at us. He seemed jumpy.

It shouldn't have been alarming. I had been told that people stared at foreigners all the time in China. You get annoyed by it or you get used to it, but you don't worry about it. Mark, however, seemed to sense that there was something different about the man behind the newspaper. And after a while, I began to think that he might be right.

When we asked for our check, the man asked for his, too. After paying, we gathered our things, exited the restaurant, and started up the hill toward our hotel. I glanced back, and there the man was, emerging from the restaurant. He looked up and down the dimly lit street for a moment and then set off in our direction.

Mark passed the word around our group that there was a suspicious stranger following us, and soon everyone was looking back over their shoulders. When we reached the hotel, one of the girls in our group, Teresa, dropped back to walk beside me.

"I feel like he's looking at me," she said. "Will you walk me to my room?"

"Of course," I said.

We split off from the rest of the group, and the man followed after us. When we climbed the stairs and turned onto Teresa's hallway, the stranger did likewise, staying about twenty yards behind us. Teresa's room was now coming up on our right, but it no longer seemed like a good idea to go there.

"Just walk past your room." I whispered. "Don't even look at it."

Teresa laughed nervously, and we kept walking. There was another staircase in front of us, and we descended to the floor below. There, we walked down the hallway and stopped in front of a random room as if preparing to enter it. The sound of footsteps echoed behind us in the stairwell.

I kept talking nervously to Teresa, trying to keep up the appearance that we were having a casual conversation. A moment later, the man emerged from the stairwell. I looked into his eyes, and he stopped. Then, seeming to have made a decision, he started moving again—and went back down the stairs.

Teresa and I stood there for a few more minutes in the vacant hallway, hardly daring to breathe, listening as the man's footsteps faded. There was no doubt about it: He had been following us. After waiting a while longer to be sure that he wasn't coming back, we went up the other staircase, and I dropped Teresa off at her room at last.

Feeling like a hero, I patrolled the halls for a few more minutes before heading back to my own room. I told Patrick what had happened. Neither of us knew what to make of it. Was the man just some harmless guy who wanted to get a closer look at a pretty foreign girl—which sounded creepy enough—or did he have more sinister intentions?

We would never find out. The next morning, we left at three o'clock to head back to Shanghai, where we would catch our return flight. The tiny bread loaf vans were waiting for us, with those dreaded hard seats and nonexistent leg space. Somehow, after a week of being a spy for Christ, I was able to handle it better this time.

When I got home, I was bursting with excitement. I shared with my friends and supporters how hungry the Chinese students had been to hear the Gospel. I told everyone who would listen about the students who had inquired about the motto "In God We Trust," and the boy who had asked me for words of hope.

But as I recounted my stories, a small voice in my head whispered that maybe those students had been toying with me. So many foreigners in China were missionaries who sought every opportunity to share the Gospel. Could it have become a running joke among the students there that you could get an American fired up by asking him about Jesus? Perhaps they had all returned to their rooms and snickered at my obsession with an obscure Jew who had lived two thousand years ago in the Middle East.

I suppressed that voice and resolved to pray for those hungry students. I took out the money that they had given me, wrote their names on the bills, and taped them to the wall by my bed. Every night, I read their names and asked God for their salvation, confident that he would hear me and work miracles in their lives.

The trip had lasted only a week, but it left a deep impression on me. My experiences confirmed everything I'd heard about China, and I felt keenly the weight of that moral obligation to intervene on behalf of the oppressed masses there. I knew now how I was going to fulfill my childhood vow to God: I would be a missionary to China.

6

A Crisis of Faith

The jogging path around Rice University was three miles long. In the spring, I began using it regularly, and as I ran, I counted in time with my steps. I recited numbers forward and backward, in ones, fives, tens, and twenties—all in Mandarin. In the year and a half that remained before I would graduate, I was determined to build as much as I could on the lesson that Andy and David had given me in that pagoda.

Numbers, of course, were not enough. I went to the language lab at Rice and explored the Chinese software. There was a program that would record your voice and then grade your pronunciation. I shouted the word for "sorry" into the microphone just as two Chinese girls were walking by. They jumped, looked at me wide-eyed, and then burst into laughter.

Spring gave way to summer, and both Mark and Nellie returned. They were planning to do a second year in China, and they would once again be raising support. I might have tried to avoid them, but that wasn't possible since we all attended the same church. Besides, I was over the previous year's incident, and I was happy to resume our friendship. Thus, almost inevitably, I again found myself having lunch with Mark—and it turned out that he had some big news to share.

"Nellie and I broke up," he said.

I stared blankly at him. When they had resumed their relationship the year before, I had regarded the transaction as final. I had reviewed the evidence and concluded that yes, they were a perfect match for each other. And then I had spent a whole year trying to move on. This sudden announcement of a second breakup threatened to undo the emotional progress I had made. I didn't know what to say except to ask *why* they had broken up. And Mark told me.

While in China, they had been in different cities, so they had communicated by phone most of the time. During one call, Nellie announced to Mark that she thought it would be nice to see other people. Mark was not happy about the proposal, and a lengthy discussion ensued. In the middle of it, Nellie received a call from someone else, and she put Mark on hold. When she came back, she told Mark that the caller was a guy, and he was asking her out on a date.

"I think I'll accept," she said. "Hold on."

Again, she put Mark on hold. An hour passed, and still

he waited, knowing that his girlfriend was planning a date with another guy—and clearly talking about a lot more besides. Eventually, Mark decided that Nellie had forgotten he was waiting, and he hung up. After that, it had hardly seemed necessary to say, "Let's break up."

Mark's story sounded humiliating, and I found myself trying to console him, though at this point the ordeal was several months in the past. Still, despite his feelings, and despite the evidence that Nellie might not make the best of girlfriends, as far as I was concerned, there was only one important piece of information in everything he had said: Nellie was available again.

After what I deemed to be a tactful amount of time—two days, perhaps—I gave Nellie a call, and we met at the House of Pies for an evening breakfast. She still didn't seem interested in anything beyond friendship; but between her breakup with Mark and our common interest in China, I suspected that God was working to bring us together.

"What's your plan for the future?" I asked over a plate of *huevos rancheros*.

"Seminary," she replied.

Stirring my eggs with my fork, I turned her answer over in my mind. In our community, there weren't many women who went to seminary. Only one of the eight full-time staff at our church was female, and she wasn't allowed to preach—or to have any authority beyond the affairs of women and children. If Nellie wanted to go to seminary, it was for her love of theology.

"And after seminary?" I asked.

"China," she said.

On a later date, Nellie revealed that she wanted to begin studying Biblical Greek on her own in order to get a head start before seminary. This reminded me not just of my own endeavor to study Chinese independently, but also of the two and a half years of ancient Greek that I had taken at Rice out of a desire to read the New Testament in its original language. Truly, Nellie and I were kindred spirits.

"That's awesome," I said. I then went on at length about my own history with Greek. I wanted her to see the significance of our common interests, and I hoped to impress her with my devotion to Biblical scholarship. When I mentioned a Greek primer that I had bought for myself, she interrupted me.

"Could I borrow it?" She asked.

"Of course," I said.

To my mind, lending Nellie a book was symbolic of forming a deeper bond with her. *This is going well*, I thought. I gave it to her a few days later, and she covered it with brown paper in that familiar way. She would be taking it to China, after all, and since it was related to Christianity, it had to be disguised.

Before Nellie left at the end of the summer, I took her out one last time. I told her that I wanted to be more than friends, and I asked her to pray for God's guidance in our relationship. Reluctance and disinterest were plain on her face, but she nodded.

"I will," she said.

And then she was gone.

Throughout the fall, I continued to court her from afar. In addition to emails, I sent a letter proclaiming my love, and I even wrote a short note in Biblical Greek. That, I figured, had to be a significant turn-on for any seminary-bound missionary girl. With prayer and persistence, I knew that it would only be a matter of time before she came around.

It was just before Christmas, and I was sitting at my desk, when an email from her appeared in my inbox. My heart fluttered, and my hands trembled as I moved my mouse to click on it. The message was short, and I found myself reading it over and over again: "I've been praying about our relationship," she wrote. "But I'm not sensing anything from Him. So I'm going to stop now."

I felt an urge to vomit.

This was worse than when Mark had announced the restoration of their relationship the year before. Then, I had been able to tell myself that her choice had little to do with me. Mark had simply been a better match for her, and they had a history together besides. But this time, the only possible conclusion was that she just wasn't attracted to me.

My ego wilted.

A future with Nellie now seemed impossible, but my interest in China remained undiminished. My final semester in college had now arrived, and as I finished up a double major in physics and math, I began thinking about how exactly I would go there. There was, of course, Cru, which I had gone with before—and which Nellie was with now. My other options, as I saw them, were to go independently or to find another organization.

I searched for weeks, and I eventually came across a group that was radically different from Cru. It was called Educational Services International—ESI for short—and it sent Christian English teachers to eleven different closed countries. The beauty of it was that they were open about their faith; there were no false pretenses, covert activities, or secret codes. Based on what I'd learned from my friends in Cru, that was impossible. But ESI was doing it.

I sent in an application.

Two weeks later, I received a phone call. ESI wanted to schedule an interview with me. I agreed, and I soon found myself talking to the president of the organization, a grandfatherly guy named Ron. We talked about my interest in missions and my experience serving the church, and I felt a good vibe. *I wouldn't mind working for this guy*, I thought.

Then, near the end of the interview, Ron asked a question that seemed to have some special significance. "You do know we have a policy that you're not allowed to date a local during your first year with us, right?"

"That won't be a problem," I said.

After going through five years of college without a girlfriend—never mind that I had spent two of them pining after Nellie—how difficult could one more year be? Add to that the fact that I found Chinese accents unattractive, and it was clear that there was no cause for concern.

"Good," said Ron. "We'll get back to you in a couple of weeks."

With that, the interview was over.

All of these developments—my progress in Mandarin, my rejection by Nellie, and my application to ESI—occurred against the backdrop of my most important endeavor of all: the continued pursuit of God himself. Every day, I was poring over the scriptures and praying. Every week, I was attending church services and Bibles studies. And whenever I could, I was reading apologetics.

The purpose of studying apologetics was to equip oneself for sharing the Gospel. We are told by the Apostle Peter, "Always be prepared to articulate a defense to everyone who asks you the reason for the hope that is within you." But for me—and many others, I suspect—it was also an effort to convince myself of things that I had never quite fully accepted.

The canonical scientific view of natural history—that the earth was old and that humans were the product of evolution—still felt right to me. The evidence appeared strong. But I was surrounded by people who insisted that the Gospel only made sense within a young-earth creationist worldview. This was an issue that had been troubling me to varying degrees since the beginning; and I was becoming ever more desperate to resolve it.

There were only two outcomes that could satisfy me. One would be to reach the conclusion that faith and evolution were compatible—that the Gospel was perfectly valid under a metaphorical interpretation of Genesis. The other would be to determine that the evolutionist worldview was in fact false. On the surface, the first of these seemed like an easy conclusion to reach. But no matter how hard I tried, I couldn't get there.

The Fall of man was an essential prerequisite for the necessity of salvation. But if we were a product of evolution, then what was sin but a natural component of our animal nature? At what point in our development could the Fall be said to have occurred, and how could we be held responsible for it? Furthermore, if death and suffering had been around before humanity arose, how could they be seen as consequences of our sin? The more I thought about it, the more I became convinced that if evolution *were* true, the Gospel could *not* be.

As I struggled with these questions, an elder at my church named Herb announced that he was going to make a presentation in my Sunday school class about the shortcomings of evolution. Though he wasn't a scientist, he was regarded as an expert in the subject, and he had been refining this presentation over a period of many years. People I respected assured me that I would be impressed.

When the day came, I sat in the front row and listened intently. At the climax of the presentation, Herb showed a drawing of a prehistoric animal with half-formed wings. "Look at this guy," he said. "These wings don't give him any kind of survival advantage at all. He's lunch!" Herb then closed with a declaration that the theory of evolution was on its last legs. In the next ten or twenty years, it would be abandoned by all mainstream scientists. His confidence was contagious, and everyone around me seemed convinced.

I felt the visceral appeal of Herb's arguments. It *did* seem inconceivable that something as complex as a wing or an eye could evolve without being directed by a force that somehow "knew" what the end product would be. How *could* the initial stages of these structures confer a survival advantage? Purely naturalistic macroevolution *had* to be impossible, I thought.

Deep down, I recognized this reasoning as unsound. There were, however, more sophisticated arguments based on the same principle. Michael Behe, a biochemist, had identified "irreducibly complex" systems, which he claimed could not have evolved by natural selection. He only gave a handful of examples, but I clung to them; they were the gaps in which my god now resided, and I was desperate to protect them.

One day, when I was searching online for data that would support my desired conclusion, I saw a link to an article that favored evolution. I stared at it for a moment, and I suddenly realized that in all my "research," I had only been reading material written by Christians. It occurred to me that if I wanted to be intellectually honest, I should examine arguments from the other side of the debate as well.

Already, my heart was pounding. I knew what I would find if I clicked on the link, and I suspected that it would convince me. To someone who had devoted his life to the Gospel, this was the most frightening kind of forbidden fruit there was. One could recover from all other sins—even adultery and murder—but to lose one's faith was to lose one's reason to live.

I clicked on the link.

My eyes traced the lines of text almost involuntarily, and ice formed in my gut. Whereas most of the apologetics materials I had read on evolution were written by lay people—well-educated Christians who fancied themselves experts—this article was written by an actual evolutionary biologist. And it was immediately clear that she had a much deeper understanding of the subject than the authors I was accustomed to reading.

She directly refuted the very examples of irreducibly complex systems to which I had been clinging, and she described in great detail how each system could plausibly have evolved gradually, such that every step would provide some small advantage. At the end of the article, she demolished the "myth" that evolution was a dying theory. Creationists had been saying this, she wrote, for decades—but in fact, the theory was only growing stronger.

The author provided links to other sources, and I soon found myself reading a multitude of articles that made all the apologists I'd ever read look like a ragtag gaggle of toddlers mounting a delusionally optimistic assault on the U.S. Navy. In that one evening, it became clear to me that evolution was simply a fact. It didn't explain the ultimate origin of life or the rise of consciousness, but it fit perfectly with geology and the rest of science to explain how life had developed once it had gotten started.

In the weeks that followed, I couldn't stop thinking about what I had learned. I wondered how much it implied about my beliefs. Were they *all* wrong, or just some of them? Were they true, but only in a metaphorical sense? And if so, why share the Gospel? It was the core of my faith, and in my view its importance depended on the literal facts of sin, salvation, and heaven. Without those things, what would be the point?

Feeling as if I were hanging from the edge of a cliff, I shifted my grip from one feeble branch to another. I tried to focus on my own conversion experience rather than worry myself with scientific questions. On that day when I had prayed with Joseph, I had felt something real. And since then, I had been transformed into a more joyful person. I had seen others, too, transformed by the Gospel. And then there were the apostles, the martyrs: Would they have died for something they knew to be a lie?

Surely Christ had indeed risen from the dead, and nothing else mattered. I kept telling myself this, but the seeds of doubt had already taken root. My confidence in my own cosmic purpose was wavering, and the practical concerns of life weighed more heavily on me. The unshakable sense of peace that I had enjoyed for so long began to crumble.

As I was moving out of my dorm after graduation, a box slid off of my car and broke open on the pavement, spilling the artifacts of my life out onto the ground.

"God damn it!" I snapped.

When the words reached my ears, my heart froze. It was a curse I hadn't uttered in five years. I had come to believe that anyone who habitually said even, "Oh, my God!" wasn't a true Christian, for to do so was to break the Third

Commandment; and if that was something you did lightly, then surely you didn't know God. I was horrified to find that such words could emerge from my own mouth. Was I myself no longer a true Christian?

The question put me in a state of crisis. It was the state I was in when I received my acceptance letter from ESI. It was the state I was in when I sent in my reply, making the commitment to serve with them in China for the coming year. And it was the state I was in several weeks later when I arrived at the campus of William Carey International University in Pasadena, California, where ESI's seven-week training program was held.

The place hardly deserved to be called a university, much less an international one. Its campus covered a mere city block, and a quarter of it had been turned into a middle school, while the main teaching building was being rented out to a local high school. Apart from that, there were only offices, a library, and dormitories—and even some of those were being rented out like apartments. But nestled as it was at the foot of the San Gabriel Mountains and blanketed with green grass, palm trees, and vibrant flowers, the campus felt like a little slice of heaven. There, surrounded by fellow believers, I hoped to experience a resurgence of faith.

7

No Turning Back

One by one, the veteran teachers stood before us and recounted tales from abroad. Some told their own stories, and others gave accounts of teachers who—often for disturbing reasons—were no longer with ESI. I noticed four main themes in their narratives: monster teammates, crumbling friendships, culture shock, and tragedy.

One teacher had received an absurd, rancorous letter from her teammate, lambasting her for leaving a dishcloth wadded up on their kitchen counter rather than hanging it up to dry. Another teacher described the process by which two of her fellow missionaries had gone from being best friends to vowing that they would hate each other for the rest of their lives. Yet another had died of meningitis.

There was only one story that wasn't depressing. It was about a guy who, after a long and demoralizing bout with diarrhea in a public restroom in China, discovered that there was no toilet paper. After an agonizing period of deliberation, he had ended up using his socks.

The purpose of sharing these stories with the new recruits was to knock down any high expectations we might have had. In fact, ESI's unofficial motto was, "Low expectations." The reason was simple: Living abroad as part of a small team wasn't easy, and ESI's leaders wanted to ensure that we approached the endeavor with a healthy amount of fear.

It worked.

As I listened to the stories, my naïve fantasy of blithely prancing hand-in-hand with fellow missionaries through fields of Chinese dandelions gave way to a nightmarish vision of psychotic teammates bursting through my bedroom ceiling in the dead of night to carve out my larynx with a rusty hedge trimmer. The only remaining spark of hope came from the realization that despite their horrific stories, these teachers *had* made the decision to come back for another year. Unless they were all masochists, this must have meant that *something* about their experiences had been rewarding.

What frightened me most was that the tales of ruined relationships were being told by people who had been placed with exactly the teammates they had requested. The lesson I took away from this was that I couldn't trust myself to choose a teammate. And yet I would have to do precisely that. One of my most important tasks during the next few weeks would be to get to know the other teachers and decide which of them I wanted to spend the year with.

I examined the people around me closely. There was my roommate, Sam, who was an accountant and a bookworm. He kept a spreadsheet of all the thousands of books he'd ever read, and he spent so much time reading on the toilet that we started calling the bathroom "Sam's office."

Then there was Ruth, a public school English teacher in her twenties who was taking a year off for missions. She often wore a shirt that said, "Instant human. Just add coffee." She was smart, pretty, and funny, but I also found her intimidating.

Erin and Amanda, two linguistics majors from the same university, were inseparable friends; it was hard to imagine them fighting. I wasn't sure I wanted them on my team, though, because they seemed to be die-hard feminists. Feminism wasn't something I'd seen in a Christian community before. The congregation I'd been part of in college had always abided by the verse stating that women shouldn't be allowed to speak in "the assembly."

The one person I could imagine turning into a monster was a guy named Jack. He was a returning teacher whose teammate from the previous year had decided not to come back. That, I figured, was a red flag right there. And although Jack seemed nice enough, he had a disconcerting way of looking at you that made you feel as if a large amount of calculation was going on behind his eyes—and nothing in his face gave any hint as to what the outcome of that calculation was.

Of course, there were other components of the training program besides choosing our teammates. One of the foremost was studying the art of teaching English. I was surprised to learn that there was actually a significant amount of theory and research behind it. Despite having considered becoming a high school physics teacher, a part of me had always thought that teachers were little more than warm bodies whose primary task consisted of turning to the right page in the teacher's edition of a textbook. But in reality, nothing could be further from the truth.

During the daytime training sessions, we learned the principles of planning effective lessons and assessing student learning outcomes; and during the evenings, we exercised our new skills in a "practicum," which consisted of teaching real ESL classes at a local church. It was quite nerve-wracking to be given a lesson topic in the afternoon and to have to create materials and present the lesson just a couple of hours later— all while being evaluated by a veteran teacher.

The third component of our training involved studying the countries in which we would be serving. I entered the first of these lessons with confidence. I had been to China and had studied the language; and for years I had been tightly integrated with a community that included a large number of Chinese Americans, as well as missionaries who had lived in China. So when the lesson began, I was shocked to discover how little I really knew.

I could have told you that around 1980, elementary school students across the country had been charged with the task of killing houseflies as part of a massive public health initiative, and that the students who brought the greatest number of dead flies to school were awarded prizes. But I couldn't name the current leader of China.

My ignorance was further exposed when we were divided into pairs and asked to conduct little debates. One person was to push the merits of the "Three-Self Churches," while the other had to argue in favor of the unregistered churches, or "house churches." The question we had to answer was which type of church was more legitimate. I was assigned to be an advocate for the Three-Self Church.

I had a vague idea—and only because the facilitator had just explained it—that the Three-Self Churches were the ones that had registered with the government. But beyond that, I didn't know much at all. I didn't even know what "Three-Self" meant. Without bothering to ask anyone, I concocted a vague but plausible understanding of "Three-Self" as an awkward reference to the trinity. This turned out to be wrong.

It took me a while to realize that the Three-Self Churches were the ones about which my friends in Cru had warned me—the ones with incomplete Bibles and sermons that were censored by party officials. Why anyone would choose to attend such a church was beyond me. But it was just now dawning on me that since ESI's philosophy was to be aboveboard in all that it did, I would be expected to participate in the Three-Self Churches rather than the house churches.

I wasn't sure how I felt about that.

I didn't have time for second thoughts, though. Training

kept me busy, and before I knew it, the time for team formation had arrived. In preparation for it, the staff gave us a questionnaire and a personality test. The questionnaire asked simple things, such as, "Is your room usually neat or messy?" It was just like the one I'd filled out for my first roommate assignment in college.

Everyone's responses, along with our pictures, were compiled into a catalog that was copied and distributed. With the aid of this catalog, we were to make three lists: people we would like to work with; people we definitely did *not* want as teammates; and people we weren't sure about. Those lists would then be used by a committee to decide our fates.

The night before our lists were due, I sat down in my dorm and, filled with the fear of God, scrutinized everyone's profile. I saw that a guy named Richard had written, "I refuse to be on the same team as a Catholic because Catholics are idolaters and idolatry is the worst sin."

Those words didn't square with what I knew of Richard. He was the gentlest person I'd ever met, and I never would have thought him capable of writing anything so harsh. I might have seen his statement as a red flag, except that I agreed with him. Catholics *were* idolaters. I put Richard on my "yes" list.

Then there were the feminists. Seeing too much potential for conflict, I put them on my "no" list. Jack went on my "no" list as well, and not just because of his disconcerting way of staring at people. I also thought that he looked a little psychotic in his profile photo. His eyes were frighteningly wide, and his hair was standing straight up in the front—a tell-tale indicator of psychosis if ever there was one.

It took me a couple of hours to go through the whole packet and give each person a "yes," "no," or "maybe." Nearly every decision was agonizing. Despite having spent several weeks together, I hadn't really gotten to know everyone that well, so I just had to go by my gut feeling and by what they had written about themselves. Because of that, a lot of people ended up on my "maybe" list.

When I finished, I surveyed my lists. I thought about what I had learned from all of the horror stories, and I was once again overcome by the feeling that I couldn't judge people accurately. I re-examined the "no" list and started second-guessing myself. Had I really put Jack on there because he looked psychotic in his picture? On second thought, that didn't seem like a very good reason. I moved him over to my "maybe" list, and then I put my pencil down.

It was all up to God now.

The next day, a committee was elected to choose the teams. It was mostly staff members and veteran teachers, but as a matter of policy, two rookies had to be included as well. I ended up being one of them. At noon, we armed ourselves with everyone's lists and a map of China, and we shut ourselves in a conference room to commence the team formation process.

We began by sifting through all the lists and identifying the people who seemed the most difficult to please—that is, the ones who had long "no" lists. Then we simply started teaming teachers up with people on their "yes" lists. It seemed easy at first; but about halfway through, we began running out of options for the people who hadn't yet been assigned a team, and we had to start moving people around.

After three hours, we placed the final name on the map and then stepped back to survey our work. I was paired with Richard. There were several non-ideal combinations, though, meaning that three or four teachers were on teams with people on their "no" lists. I would have thought the best way to proceed would be to make small adjustments until a better arrangement was reached. But Linda, our leader, had us start over from scratch.

The second configuration took longer, but it appeared to be much better than the first. Linda still wasn't satisfied, though, and we started over yet again. When we finished the third configuration, the sun was rising. Exhausted, I looked at the map. One girl had been put with someone on her "no" list, but it was a four-person team, and the other two people were on her "yes" list. It seemed the best we could do, and Linda finally announced that we were done.

Our fates were now set.

The committee had decided that I would go to Beijing, where I would be teaching at the Sinopec Management Institute. My teammate was going to be Jack—who now informed me that he preferred to be called Hudson. I looked at his picture again and wondered whether it had been a good idea to move him from my "no" list to my "maybe" list. Surely he wasn't really psychotic. And perhaps I was only imagining those calculations behind his eyes.

It was soon time for the teams to depart for their respective countries. Over a period of two days, a different group left every four or five hours. Those of us going to China would be the last to leave, so I merely watched and waited as the others trickled out of William Carey International University. They rolled their luggage into the rec center and sat down, talking nervously. Then, when the time came, they boarded a bus and left for the airport.

Most of them I would never see again.

When our turn arrived, it was dark outside; and with our departure, the campus was left silent and empty. On the bus ride, others talked excitedly; but I sat quietly, looking out the window, realizing that the point of no return was quickly approaching. As a missionary, I would finally be fulfilling my vow to God, and that gave me a sense of relief. But at the same time, my doubts about the truth of the Gospel continued to churn within me—and a part of me wondered whether going to China might turn out to be the biggest mistake of my life.

8

A Second First Impression

It was early on a Tuesday morning when we landed in Beijing. My mind was numb with disbelief—not so much that I was in China, but that I was there to *stay*. As our group stepped out of the airport and into the swarm of taxi drivers who were vying for our attention, my first thought was that there was no sky. The city was encased in a confining, gray-brown cocoon of smog.

I didn't have time for many other thoughts, because I was preoccupied with keeping track of my luggage as we were herded toward a pair of buses. I boarded one and sat near the back, next to one of the veteran teachers, a guy named Ken who had told me that he always introduced himself to his new students by informing them that he was in his forties and was still a virgin. Apart from that, we really didn't know each other very well.

"Did you say you'd been to China before?" Ken asked.

"Yes," I replied.

"And what were you doing?"

I opened my mouth to tell him that I had come on a mission trip, but then I stopped. I looked up at the ceiling of the bus, the cracked vinyl paneling above the windows, and the grimy air conditioning vents. Could there be a bug hidden up there? Was some Chinese official listening to us?

"I was visiting a friend who was studying Chinese," I said at last, thinking of Mark.

The buses took us to a building that was labeled "Foreign Experts" in giant red characters. Ordinarily, English teachers weren't designated as Foreign Experts, but ESI had some *guanxi*—connections—with the right authorities and had been able to secure official Expert status for us. As we checked in, we were given red lanyards that said "Certificate of Experts" in large, gold letters.

Hudson and I were assigned a room on the fourteenth floor, and we went to drop off our bags. I felt like it should be nighttime—we had just finished a long journey and were checking into a hotel—but a look out the window showed that the day was just beginning.

Apart from the smog and the billboards, it was like the China of so many fantasies. Down on our right was a garden filled with trees, flowering bushes, and winding paths. To the left was a courtyard where people were practicing Tai Chi in formation, some of them holding swords. Perhaps the stereo-type was true, I thought, and all Chinese people were masters of martial arts.

Our group spent two days touring Beijing's major attractions, including the Forbidden City and the Summer Palace. Then, on the third morning, the individual teams began leaving one by one as their schools' Foreign Affairs Officers—FAO, for short—arrived to take them to the cities where they would be teaching.

Since Hudson and I were already in our destination city, our FAO was one of the first to show up. His name was Mr. Ji. A nervous, balding man with a comb-over and a perpetually strained look of emotional constipation in his eyes, he greeted us cordially and helped us load our luggage into a van with a driver who sat waiting, a cigarette hanging from his lips.

"I think you are tired," Mr. Ji said.

"Yes," I answered.

Neither of us could think of anything else to say.

As we drove, I stared at everything we passed. Under a highway overpass, some elderly men sat in rickety wooden chairs, getting their hair cut by a couple of leathery-skinned old barbers. They looked like relics of a bygone age, taken by surprise as the modern city of Beijing had sprung up around them. Hudson attempted to make conversation with Mr. Ji, but after only about two minutes, the van stopped in front of a gray building.

"We are here," Mr. Ji said.

He took us inside and up an elevator to the eighth floor to show us our rooms. They were like hotel rooms, with tiny bathrooms that had no enclosed shower or tub, but instead a small heated water tank with a shower head on it mounted over the sink. I had seen one before, when I stayed with my brother in Argentina; he had called it "the widow-maker" because of the potential for electrocution.

We left our luggage in our rooms, and Mr. Ji took us down three floors to show us our office and classrooms. Then he walked us over to an adjacent building and pointed out a small cafeteria. With that, the tour was over. He returned us to our rooms, handed us his business card, and backed hurriedly into the elevator like a spooked crab retreating into its hole.

That quickly, Hudson and I were alone.

We looked around our living area. It was separated from the rest of the eighth floor by a metal security door with an electronic lock. Mr. Ji had given us each a key, which looked like a large watch battery. What I didn't like was that we had to use the key to get *out* as well as in. It seemed like a safety hazard. However, there was a staircase that was accessible from the back of our living area. We descended the seven flights to the ground floor, where we found a pair of emergency exit doors. They were chained shut.

"I can't believe this," I said.

"It's normal in China," Hudson said, subtly reminding me that he had already spent a year in the country. So much of what was new to me was familiar and downright boring to him. But I wasn't prepared to be put in danger just because it was "normal" to chain emergency exits here.

"Well, I'm going to have them take the chain off."

"Ha!" Hudson laughed. "Good luck."

We climbed back to the eighth floor and explored a bit more before finally setting to work. Being young bachelors, we hadn't packed much, so moving in was a small job. It was unpacking the materials in our office that would take time. The room was filled with cabinets and taped-up boxes; and everything—floor, desks, boxes, shelves, and all—was covered in a thick blanket of dust. Within seconds, my eyes were itching and my nose was running.

"This is *years'* worth of dust!" I exclaimed.

Again, Hudson laughed. "No, no. This is China. Dust collects faster here. It's just one summer's worth. Trust me."

We spent the afternoon unpacking books, audiotapes, board games, dishes, kitchen utensils, and packets of food that had been brought from America by previous teachers. Then, after an early dinner, we turned our attention to our dorm rooms. Both of us were eager to check our email and contact our friends and family back home, so the first thing we did was connect our laptops to the ethernet ports. Unfortunately, they didn't work.

There was a temporary solution that ought to be simple enough. Hudson knew from his previous year in China what the characters for "internet bar" looked like—well enough to recognize them if he saw them, at any rate. He described one of them to me, saying that it looked like an open mouth viewed from the side, and we set out into the neighborhood in search of it.

An hour passed before we broke down and decided to ask for help. On the sidewalk in front of our school, there were a few locals who were standing around, chatting and smoking. One of them was guy running a small fruit stand. It seemed reasonable to suppose that he would know his way around the area.

"Let's start with him," Hudson said.

As we approached, the vendor smiled, apparently eager to do business with a couple of foreigners. I thought about how best to inquire about an internet bar using my limited vocabulary and settled on a line that seemed appropriate. I rehearsed it a few times in my head and then, in slow, exaggerated tones, spoke it aloud.

"We will get online," I said.

The man's smile faltered.

Although Hudson knew what the characters for "internet bar" looked like, neither of us knew how to say them. I had, however, learned how to say "get online" in my introductory Chinese course the year before, and I was quite sure that what I was saying would suffice for our present purposes. Unfortunately, I had not yet mastered the subtle difference between two different words for "want"—one of which means "would like to," and the other of which, the way I was using it, means "will."

"We will get online!" I said again, imagining that if I repeated myself emphatically enough, the meaning would get through. But no matter how many times I said it, the fruit vendor didn't seem to understand. So after about a minute of this, I decided to change tactics. I knew how to say "where is the" and "to get online." So I put these phrases together and tried again.

"Where is the to get online?" I asked.

As I repeated this second question, a small crowd gathered. The other vendors and locals had seen that something strange was going on, and they came over, either to gawk at the psychotic foreigner who was yelling at a fruit vendor about getting online or to attempt to decipher my meaning and help us. Soon the situation had evolved into a big game of charades, with me typing on an imaginary keyboard, spouting nonsense about the internet. I tried every combination of words I could think of.

"We will use a computer!" I shouted.

The onlookers narrowed their eyes and scratched their chins.

"WHERE IS THE COMPUTER?" I demanded.

After this last question, a woman in the crowd finally spoke to us.

"Computer?" she asked in English.

"Yes, computer!" I replied. Hudson and I cheered, and several of the people around us joined in celebrating what seemed to be a momentous breakthrough in international relations. "We want to find a computer," I told the woman.

"Computer?" she asked again.

"Yes. Computer."

She took out her car keys and pointed first at us and then at a little black Volkswagen parked at the curb. I stared for a moment, wondering what she was trying to tell us. Did she just happen to have a computer in her car?

"I think she's offering us a ride," Hudson said.

Feeling slightly guilty for troubling her but grateful for her help, we climbed into her car, and she began driving. We didn't consider at all the question of how unwise it might be to get into a car with a stranger in a foreign country; but she was the only person who appeared to have a clue what we wanted. She was our Good Samaritan.

We drove for some time. The sun had just been setting when we got in the car, but the sky was now completely dark. After a while, I started thinking, "Surely there is a net bar closer than this." Meanwhile, our driver was making calls on her cell phone and signaling for other drivers to roll down their windows so she could ask them—as it seemed to me, at least—where she could take us to find a computer. She was evidently working quite hard on our behalf, and I appreciated her dedication.

Eventually, she stopped the car in front of a building and pointed at it triumphantly. Hudson and I stared, trying to figure out what it was. All over the side of the building were enormous advertisements—for computers.

"I think this is a computer *store*," Hudson said.

After he had said so, it seemed obvious. It *was* a store— and it was closed. Feeling extra guilty now for accidentally misleading our generous benefactor, I explained that we did not want to *buy* a computer; we just wanted to write email. Understanding illuminated her face, and she ushered us back into her car. Feeling encouraged, I attempted to make light banter in Chinese as we continued driving.

"What kind of work do you do?" I asked.

"Driving," she replied. She took her hands off the steering wheel and mimed the act of turning an imaginary steering wheel in the air above the real one. I was confused. *What does she mean?* I thought. Perhaps she drove a bus. Or maybe a taxi. Thinking the matter to be an interesting question, I shared it with Hudson.

"She said her job is to drive," I said.

Hudson groaned.

"What?" I asked.

"This is her taxi," he said.

"But it's not a taxi."

"It's an illegal one," he said. "She's going to charge us."

It all made sense, and just like that, whatever small triumphs I'd had earlier were crushed under the weight of this revelation. For the remainder of the ride, I made no more attempts at banter. When she finally stopped the car in front of an internet bar—this time we saw and recognized the characters—I asked her, "How much?"

"Fifty," she said.

At the current exchange rate, that amounted to about six dollars. I felt certain that she was ripping us off, but in fact it wasn't that much, even by Chinese standards, considering how long and how far she had taken us. After I handed over the money, she took out a piece of paper, wrote three Chinese characters on it, and handed it to me.

"What is this?" I asked.

"It's where you live."

It turned out to be the name of a bridge near the Sinopec campus. She had written it down so that when we were done checking our email, we could show it to another taxi driver and would be able to get home. So she actually cared.

The next day, we set out on foot again and finally found an internet café in our neighborhood. It was a twenty-minute walk from our campus, which wasn't too bad, and we began making the trek every evening after dinner.

With our routine thus established, there now remained only one more order of business to attend to before classes started. Hudson had left two bags of his belongings in the city of Tai'An, where he had been teaching the previous year, and he needed to go pick them up if he wanted to have clothes to wear. So we took an overnight train that weekend to retrieve them.

It was a mostly quiet trip. On the way there, Hudson's face was splattered with feces—not his own—by a malfunctioning toilet. In a garden at Hudson's former school, a toothless old man walked up to me and fondled my nose. And on the way back, a girl named Bibo, who said that she was on her way to Beijing to visit her boyfriend—who, she felt it necessary to emphasize for some reason, was quite ugly—asked me for my phone number.

When we returned to Beijing, Hudson and I picked up

right where we'd left off. During the day, we planned our lessons; and in the evening, we walked to the internet bar to check our email. An entire month would pass before we would discover that there was a computer lab with internet access, free for us to use, on the Sinopec campus, right next to the cafeteria. Evidently, Mr. Ji hadn't thought we'd be interested in it.

9

Teaching the Dead

The sudden ringing of our office phone startled us both. Until now, we had barely noticed that our office *had* a phone. I looked at Hudson, shrugged, and picked up the receiver. Figuring that trying to speak Chinese would be futile, I answered with a simple hello.

"Mr. Rambow?" said a female voice.

"Yes," I replied.

"Please come to room 310."

The caller hung up, and I eyed the receiver for a moment before putting it down. I told Hudson what she had said and then took the elevator to the third floor to look for room 310. It was an office. Inside, sitting behind a desk, was a slender Chinese woman who was perhaps thirty years old. She had long, straight, raven-black hair, dark complexion, and glasses so thick that my eyes watered just looking at them.

"You called for me?" I asked.

"Yes," she said. "My name is Miss Wang." She stood and gestured toward a chair across from her desk. "Please sit down." I took the chair, and she sat back down as well.

"I have your class roster," she said.

She picked up a folder from her desk, opened it, and took out a piece of paper to hand to me. I wasn't paying attention to it, though, because something that had been under the folder caught my eye. Taped to the surface of Miss Wang's desk was a photograph of a newborn baby's penis.

Good Lord! I thought. Why would anyone want to have a picture like that taped to their desk where they would see it all the time?

As I stared, the answer occurred to me. One of my reading assignments during training had been an article about how sons were preferred over daughters in China. Baby girls were often abandoned or even murdered so the parents could try for a boy instead. This photograph indicated that someone—a relative of Miss Wang, or perhaps Miss Wang herself—was proud to have had a son.

"Here!" said Miss Wang, shaking the roster in front of me.

Putting the photograph out of mind, I took the roster and looked over it. There were fifteen students in total, and they were divided into two classes. The final name on each list had a couple of characters written beside it in parentheses. I wondered idly what they meant, thinking that perhaps those students' placement was tentative.

"Do you have any questions?" Miss Wang asked.

"No," I said.

Of course I did, though. I wanted to know what those characters meant. But for some reason, I didn't want to ask Miss Wang. I figured that I could look them up later. On hearing that I had no questions, she stood up. I stared blankly at her for a moment before realizing that this was her way of dismissing me.

When I got back to our office, I looked up the mysterious characters. They translated to "class monitor." I wasn't sure exactly what that meant, but I figured it was something along the lines of "a student who keeps an eye on everyone to make sure all of the rules are being followed and to report any violations to some higher communist authority." It was a little disturbing, but I supposed it was good to know which students would be spying on us.

The next day, we had a formal opening ceremony, at which I had to give a speech—as the elder member of our team, I was officially the leader—and then classes started at last. The curriculum consisted of four subjects: reading and writing, listening comprehension, conversational skills, and American culture. This last subject was our Trojan horse; it was designed to give us opportunities to teach the students about Christianity and find out whether any of them were interested.

Our daily schedule was simple. Classes met from eight in

the morning to eleven-thirty, and then we had lunch in the cafeteria with the students. For the first half of the morning, I taught one group while Hudson taught the other; then we switched and taught the same lessons over again. Afternoons were reserved for planning, grading, office hours, and social time with students.

At the end of the first week, Hudson and I sat down to discuss what we had learned about our students so far. I started with the obvious: They were all businessmen—well, one was a woman—who ranged in age from early twenties to late forties. I further noted that they were remarkably respectful and hospitable. One student, named Jian, had taken me shopping to make sure I knew where to get all the groceries I wanted. He had examined my shopping list and cheerfully led me up and down the aisles to find everything.

Hudson nodded when I finished talking. I detected a hint of a smug grin on his face, and I knew he was about to reveal that he had learned something I hadn't. "Do you know how many of them are Communist Party members?" he asked.

"No," I said.

"More than half."

"How do you know?"

"I asked them."

This shocked me. For some reason, I had felt that it wouldn't be a good idea to ask people whether they were in the Party. I voiced my concern, and Hudson explained that in China, the Communist Party was essentially an honor society, like Phi Beta Kappa. Our students would be happy to advertise their membership.

Hudson's revelation put me in a state of despair. I had heard that in order to join the Party, you had to sign a document renouncing belief in God. To me, that was tantamount to signing up for an eternity in hell. I had to remind myself that even a card-carrying Communist was no more spiritually dead than I myself had been before my own rebirth. God could still save them.

With this in mind, I established the habit of praying daily for all fifteen of our students by name. I prayed—as I felt I should—for opportunities to share the Gospel with them; I prayed that God would soften their hearts and show them their need for a savior; and I prayed that they would come to know him and further spread the light of Christ in China long after Hudson and I had left. These objectives constituted half of my mission.

The other half was to serve the Chinese church.

It wasn't until perhaps our third Sunday in Beijing that we at last ventured out in search of Haidian Church, the Three-Self congregation with which ESI had a longstanding relationship. The previous year's teachers had left behind written directions, saying that the church was located in a place called Haidian Book Town; so we hopped into a taxi and asked to be taken there.

Twenty minutes later, the driver dropped us off at a dirty promenade that had the feel of the grunge future depicted in science fiction stories. The street was lined with old five- and six-story buildings, their facades stained dark by years of exposure to coal smoke. The ground was littered with garbage, some of it tumbling in the wind, and the crowd was dotted with beggars clothed in grimy rags. And yet the first few floors of the buildings on either side held shops that sold state-of-the-art cell phones, cameras, and other electronics.

"Where is Haidian Book Town?" I asked a vendor.

"This is it," he said.

It turned out that the whole street was Haidian Book Town. In addition to the electronics shops, there were multiple bookstores, as well as shops that sold art supplies, musical instruments, and clothing. Near the middle of the promenade was the church. It looked no different from any of the other buildings, but it had a big red sign with a white cross on it, and there was a line of people waiting to go in.

Hudson and I queued up, and we saw that several of the beggars were working the line of churchgoers, grinning toothlessly and murmuring softly. They were especially attracted to the foreigners, of which there were a few others besides Hudson and me. We put one kuai in their cups when they approached us, and they nodded gratefully and moved on. One beggar, an old man, lay on the ground, shaking. His cup sat beside his head. He was evidently unable to move on his own, and I imagined that someone must have brought him there so he could beg. I put one kuai in his cup, too.

After a short wait, people started pouring out of the church; one service had ended, and the next was about to begin. The line began moving, and we entered the building. Ushers at the entrance handed us printed programs and directed us up some stairs. When we reached the third floor, where the service would be held, we were given tiny radio receivers with ear buds and ushered toward rows of folding chairs.

While people trickled in, a lady was teaching the congregation the hymns that would be sung during the service. She called out one line at a time, slowly and clearly, and then sang it while playing the melody on the piano. Then she motioned for the congregation to sing it with her.

Hudson and I found seats and fiddled with our radios. As we waited, another foreigner came in and sat down next to me. With a white beard and a round belly, and wearing a dingy old newsboy cap, he looked like Santa Claus on a day off. He introduced himself as Gary, and we started talking. I asked him about the Three-Self Churches, and Haidian Church in particular. I wanted to know why he chose to come here instead of BICF—the Beijing International Christian Fellowship.

"They don't let Chinese people in at BICF," he said. "But I can invite Chinese friends to this church." He further elaborated that he didn't think Jesus would have been willing to stand at the entrance to a church and turn away people who didn't have foreign passports, as was done at BICF.

"What's the theology like here?" I asked.

"It's good," he said. "They have a more orthodox interpretation of scripture here than most churches in America."

I nodded, understanding that by "orthodox" he meant conservative and evangelical, which were good qualities in a church. I also understood his sentiment about America; everyone knew that most "Christians" in America were too liberal to count as true believers.

I continued questioning Gary as we waited for the service to begin. He had been coming here for a year, often bringing Chinese friends who had expressed interest. And then after church, he always invited them over to his place to continue studying the Bible. It sounded to me like he had a fruitful ministry going, and I imagined that one day I would be doing something similar.

At eleven o'clock, the choir emerged, wearing traditional robes and singing a familiar introit as they walked to their chairs on the risers. It was a tune that I had heard at the Methodist church where I grew up. When it was over, a woman walked to the pulpit and directed us to stand, and we began singing hymns.

Everything about the service was familiar, from the hymns to the recitation of the Lord's prayer; and it suddenly felt incredible to be on the other side of the world from where I had grown up, worshiping with people whose appearance and culture were as different from my own as could be, singing the same songs, praising the same God, acting in one faith. It brought tears to my eyes.

Then came the sermon, which we heard via simultaneous translation through the receivers we had been given. I no longer remember the topic, but I considered it Biblically sound and noted that it contained a presentation of the Gospel. Clearest in my memory is the sound of the translator's voice coming through the earphones. She sounded passionate and somewhat distressed, as if she were deeply pained by the certainty that the world could not appreciate the weight of the words she was speaking.

When the service was over, two Chinese girls came to greet Gary, and he introduced them to me. One was a tall and slender girl named Jean. As soon as she spoke, there was no mistaking her voice; she had been the one translating the sermon. The other was a round-faced girl with short hair and glasses. The leader of the translation team, she had taken the English name Chanel—which I thought odd, because to me it symbolized materialism as much as a name could.

When Chanel heard that this was our first time at Haidian Church, she proceeded to give us a tour. She led us down to the second floor, where the offices and the church bookstore were located. I looked around, and I was amazed by what I saw. There were the usual trinkets you expect to find in a Christian bookstore—little plaques and key chains with Bible verses on them—and there were Bibles, some of which were bilingual.

I picked up a Bible and flipped through it to see which books were missing, but I found that they were all there. I checked a monolingual Chinese Bible and found that it, too, was complete. I bought one of the bilingual ones, and no one asked me to sign my name. Plenty of Chinese parishioners were also buying bibles without signing their names. That quickly, half of what I'd been told about China's registered churches had just been debunked.

Once the crowd had thinned, Chanel brought us to the senior pastor, Pastor Wu. He was familiar with ESI and had known that we would be coming.

"How can we serve the church?" I asked.

"Can you help our translators improve their English?"

I said that I would be happy to.

By the time I left the building, my schedule appeared to be set for every remaining Sunday that I would spend in China. I would go to the 11:00 service, eat lunch afterward with Gary and the translators, attend Gary's Bible study in his apartment in the afternoon, and help the translation team practice their English in the evening. I dove right into all of these things with gusto on that very day.

We ate at the California Beef Noodle King, which was just across the promenade from the church, and then we took a bus to Gary's apartment. I was surprised to find that it was little more than a dormitory at the university where he taught computer programming, and it was grungier by far than my room at Sinopec.

When everyone had arrived, Gary directed us all to introduce ourselves. Most of the attendees were translators from Haidian Church whom I had already met. But there were a few people I hadn't seen before. There was a guy named Glen who was known for being a good cook—he had worked in a Chinese restaurant in Scotland while going to graduate school there. And there was a quiet, pretty girl named Leila who spent the whole time staring thoughtfully at her Bible.

They were in the middle of a series of lessons on the gifts

of the Holy Spirit described in Romans 12, and Gary had prepared an activity to help us identify what our gifts were. It turned out to be nothing more than a personality test he had found online that asked how you would behave in certain situations. You just had to answer a few dozen questions and then add up some numbers in different columns. Each column corresponded to one of the gifts, and the total for that column indicated the extent to which you had that gift.

My strongest gifts were revealed to be "mercy" and "prophecy." I was sitting there contemplating the result, thinking how much better it would be to have the gift of healing, when Gary came up behind me and peeked over my shoulder.

"That's a very unusual combination," he said.

"Really?" I asked. "Why?"

Gary explained to me that prophecy generally involved relaying a message from God about what people were doing wrong. A prophet's job was to call for people to repent and to warn of God's impending judgment—like Jonah in Nineveh. Showing mercy was somewhat contrary to making proclamations of judgment, so it was unusual for the two to go together.

The gift of prophecy sounded good to me, but I wasn't very impressed by the idea of determining one's spiritual gifts by filling out a questionnaire downloaded from the internet and then adding up a bunch of numbers. Not only did it seem to me that the test merely revealed the weighting of certain natural inclinations that one might just as easily have *without* the Holy Spirit, but I also found myself thinking that spiritual gifts ought to be revealed in a more . . . I don't know . . . *spiritual* way.

After the Bible study, I relaxed for a while, grabbed dinner, and then returned to the church to meet with the translators. It turned out that most of them were college students who were majoring in English and had become Christian under the influence of a foreign teacher. I suspected that most of those teachers had been missionaries from Campus Crusade for Christ or a similar ministry. I didn't bother to ask, though, because I knew that such organizations rarely revealed their true identity to the people among whom they proselytized.

My role at the meetings would be quite simple. All they wanted was someone to practice their English with, and since their job at the church was to translate sermons, it seemed reasonable for us to read and discuss the Bible together. They especially wanted help with the pronunciation of the obscure names in the Old Testament, such as Abimelech, Manasseh, and Hezekiah. It didn't seem like very significant work, but it was what they wanted me to do; and I was there to serve them.

10

A Serious Matter

L ate one afternoon, I heard an unexpected knock at my
door. I opened it, and there before me stood Zhang and
Geng, the two class monitors. Although I had been teaching
them for weeks now, I couldn't help feeling intimidated. They
were both businessmen in their forties, and at the moment
they looked rather serious.

"We need to talk to you," said Zhang.

Uh oh, I thought. *We're in trouble for saying something
about Christianity.*

"Will you please come to Miss Wang's office?" Zhang
asked.

It didn't seem that I had much of a choice. We took the
elevator down a couple of floors, and I followed the two of

them to Miss Wang's office. When we arrived, I saw that there were several other students crowded behind Miss Wang. None of them looked happy.

"Is there a problem?" I asked.

"Yes," said Miss Wang.

Swallowing, I clenched my hands into fists to keep them from trembling visibly. Questions flooded my panicked mind. What had we done to upset them? Who had reported us? Were we going to be kicked out of the country? I waited, paralyzed, for Miss Wang to elaborate.

"It's Hudson," she said.

I exhaled in relief. It was tremendously selfish of me, but I was glad to know that *I* was not the problem—Hudson was. Still, I had plenty of reason to worry. What had he done?

"We need a different teacher," said Zhang.

"Why?" I asked. Even as the word left my mouth, my imagination began playing through the most likely scenario: Hudson had seized an opportunity to talk about Christianity in class, and one of the monitors had taken note and reported him. I wondered how they would explain the situation to me.

"He never smiles," Zhang said.

"Sometimes," added another student, "He just stands in front of the class looking at his watch."

I stared back at my students with my mouth hanging open. It had nothing to do with religion after all. And Hudson hadn't been having an affair with the female student—or any of the males, for that matter. Suddenly, I wanted to laugh. They wanted a new teacher because Hudson didn't *smile*?

Because he looked at his *watch*?

"When can ESI send a new teacher?" asked Miss Wang.

The premise of the question disturbed me: They had already made up their mind that they wanted a new teacher, and they took it for granted that ESI would send one. I was fairly sure it wasn't possible, though; and despite Hudson's mysterious calculations and occasional smug grins, I had no desire to replace him.

"Let me talk to my supervisor at ESI," I said at last.

Miss Wang nodded.

My supervisor was a teacher named Lillian who had been placed at Peking University. When I called her, I had little hope that the ordeal could end well. But she offered the simplest possible solution: Tell Miss Wang that it was ESI's policy not to replace anyone without first giving them a chance to improve. And then talk to Hudson.

The conversation with Miss Wang turned out to be easy—I had only to relay Lillian's words—but the prospect of confronting Hudson was agonizing. I prayed fervently that evening, and then I sat down with him, explained what had happened, and watched to see how he would take it.

"Yeah," Hudson said. "I've been feeling kind of depressed lately."

"Like . . . clinically depressed?" I asked.

"No. Just down about some things," he said. "I can do better."

With that, we prayed and then adjourned our little team meeting. A few days later, I took Zhang and Geng aside and asked them how they thought Hudson was doing. I braced myself for their response.

"Much better," Zhang said. He and Geng both looked impressed, and I realized that in their eyes, I was the one who had solved the problem. It felt good—though I had actually done almost nothing. Hudson was the one making the effort to change, and as long as he could maintain it, everything would be all right.

About a week later, there came another knock at my door. It was a different student this time, a skinny guy in his thirties who had taken the English name Justin. He had a perpetual glint of mischief in his eyes, and since the first day of class, I had been trying to decide whether he was a genuinely shady character or a harmless joker.

"I need to talk to you about a serious matter," he said.

Oh, no, I thought. *It's Hudson again.*

My panic must have shown on my face, because Justin held up a hand and smiled soothingly. "Take it easy," he said. Then he reached into his jacket pocket and withdrew a pencil and a writing pad. "We have decided that you need a good Chinese girl. I told my wife, and she has agreed to be your matchmaker. She is very good at it. I just need you to tell me what kind of girl you want."

It took a while for his words to sink in. Once they had, and my nightmarish vision of Miss Wang and a roomful of frowning students had faded, relief flooded over me and I burst out laughing.

"This is not a joke!" Justin said.

"I'm sorry," I said. "I was just so worried when you told me you needed to talk about something serious."

"This *is* serious!"

"You want to know what kind of girl I want?"

"Yes," he said. "You tell me how tall, what kind of personality, what major, and my wife will find her." As he finished speaking, he stood holding his pencil poised above the notepad, ready to record the qualities of the woman of my dreams. There was an eager gleam of excitement in his eyes.

It was tempting. But the text of that clause in my contract with ESI—the one stating that I wouldn't date a local during my first year in the country—floated before my eyes. I was not about to violate it. I explained this to Justin, and he wilted. The hand holding the notepad fell to his side, and he walked away looking so disappointed that I felt guilty for rejecting his services.

Just a few days later, I was eating lunch in the cafeteria when an unfamiliar student—a girl enrolled in a different program—walked over to my table and sat beside me. She looked to be just a few years older than me and had braces on her teeth, which I hadn't seen before in China.

"Hi," she said. "My name is Bonnie."

"I'm Henry," I said.

An awkward moment of silence elapsed, during which I waited passively for Bonnie to reveal her agenda. She shifted in her seat, cleared her throat, and then opened her mouth to speak again.

"Everyone says you are a very good teacher," she said. "I

hope we can be friends."

"Me too," I said, without the slightest shred of sincerity—unless "hoping that we could be friends" meant nothing more than a willingness to nod and smile whenever I passed her in the hallway.

With that, the conversation was over, and Bonnie got up and left. As soon as she was out of sight, yet another student—one of Bonnie's friends, another girl I didn't know—sat down next to me and asked what I thought of her.

"She seems nice," was all I could say.

"Do you like her?"

I opened my mouth to speak, but nothing came out.

"She likes you a lot," the girl said. Then she leaned close, and in a near whisper, added, "She has told everyone that she is going to get you to fall in love with her."

It turned out that Bonnie was indeed bent on winning my affection. She began approaching me at most meals, usually just to smile and say hello. I smiled back, uttering appropriate pleasantries. I probably ought to have indicated to her in one of those exchanges that I wasn't interested, but I just couldn't bring myself to reject her—at least, not without unintentionally leading her on for a few weeks first.

It was a Sunday evening when she came and knocked on my dormitory door. She had been gone for a few days, though I hadn't noticed, and she was ecstatic to have returned at last—because she couldn't wait to see me again.

"I have a gift for you," she said.

I did my best to feign excitement, and she held out a small

box for me to take—the sort that an engagement ring might come in. As my mind struggled to think of a gentle way to reject it, my hands reached out on their own accord and took hold of the box. I had no intention of looking inside it, though, until—

"Open it," she said.

It was too late. I opened the box and looked inside. There, resting on a tiny lace pillow, was a small, jade carving of a Buddha, tied to a red silk string. It was a pendant for me to wear around my neck. Bonnie was looking at me expectantly, likely waiting for me to put it on.

"Thank you," I said, "but I can't take this."

"It's just a gift for a friend," she said. "I'll see you tomorrow." And with that, she flashed her braces at me and walked away, leaving me standing in my doorway, looking down at the little Buddha and hoping it hadn't cost her much.

What Bonnie had no way of knowing was that where she saw a beautiful piece of jewelry, I saw a satanic idol. As soon as I had closed the door, I hurled the carving onto the tile floor as hard as I could, intending to shatter it. It ricocheted, hit the wall, and came to rest behind my bed. I picked it up, and seeing that it hadn't even sustained a scratch, I threw it again—with the same result.

I tried setting it on the floor and hitting it with the base of a brass lamp. The blow took a chip out of a floor tile but left the Buddha unscathed. I tried smashing it under a table leg, and then under the foot of my bed. But nothing worked. After thirty minutes, I gave up and threw the carving in the trash. God would have to be satisfied that I had done my best.

Bonnie only said hello to me once more after that. The sight of me not wearing the pendant was evidently enough to make her give up her pursuit. I felt guilty—it did seem a bit rude to spend half an hour trying to shatter a gift that had been tenderly offered in hopes of kindling a beautiful romance—but I didn't see that there was anything else I could have done.

My difficulties with girls soon extended beyond Sinopec. I was now attending Haidian Church alone—Hudson had started going to BICF—and I often found myself sitting beside an attractive girl who wanted to talk. I had been warned that this would happen—not because of my gorgeously chiseled face and callipygian figure, but because I was a potential ticket to America.

One morning, a pretty, copper-skinned girl with hazel eyes—the lightest color I'd ever seen on a Chinese person without contacts—sat down next to me before the service. I thought of the warnings I had received, but pushed them away. The girl had come to church on her own, after all, and it had been mere coincidence that one of the few remaining empty seats was beside me. And anyway, was it *wrong* for a girl to be interested in meeting a foreigner? She smiled warmly at me, doubling her beauty, and I smiled back.

"Do you speak English?" I asked.

She looked down, flushing slightly in embarrassment, before saying in Chinese that she didn't. This surprised me. She looked like a college student, and I knew that there wasn't a college student in China—or, for that matter, a high school student—who wasn't required to study English. Not ready to give up, I switched to my fledgling Chinese.

"Do you come here every week?" I asked.

"No, this is my first time," she answered.

"Why did you come?"

"I saw all the people going in," she said. "I was curious."

On hearing that, my missionary instinct kicked in. Anyone who entered a church out of curiosity about what went on inside clearly didn't know much about Christianity; and that probably meant that she had never heard the Gospel. Perhaps I could be the one to share it with her. Thus convincing myself that I was purely interested in her spiritual welfare, I doubled my effort to get to know her.

Her name was Xingmei, a combination of characters that essentially meant "flourishing beauty." I asked where she was from, and she told me that her hometown was Dali, in the Yunnan province. I had never heard of it, but my mind conjured an image of forested hills. An unbidden fantasy of traveling there with her began unfolding before my mind's eye. And that quickly, the Gospel had vanished from my thoughts.

The service began, and Xingmei and I turned our attention to the choir as they sang the introit and shuffled into place on the risers. When it was time for the congregation to sing, Xingmei and I shared a hymnal. We recited the Apostle's Creed, we sang the Doxology, and we said the Lord's Prayer. I watched Xingmei throughout, and it looked like all of this was new and interesting to her, as I hoped it would be. But then the sermon began.

They must have had a rule at Haidian Church that sermons had to be at least forty-five minutes long. From the translations, I gathered that they were pretty deep. They were also rife with real-life examples that I thought must resonate with Christian Chinese listeners. But I suspected that a newcomer would find them boring; and sure enough, when I looked over at Xingmei, she was shifting in her seat and glancing at the exit.

Not wanting her to be deterred on her first visit, I took it upon myself to explain things to her and keep her entertained while the pastor droned on. I didn't want to disturb anyone around us, so I took out a pad of paper to write notes to her. Soon we were passing the notepad back and forth, happily scrawling little messages to each other like a couple of kids in the back of a middle school classroom. I couldn't write more than a few Chinese characters, and she didn't know any English at all, so we ended up writing our notes in pinyin—a highly ambiguous phonetic system that's far from ideal for effective communication.

I began by trying to explain the basic tenets of Christianity—which to me meant the four spiritual laws that I'd learned in Campus Crusade for Christ—but between my limited vocabulary and the ineffectiveness of communicating in pinyin, about ninety percent of what I wanted to say came across as the written equivalent of toddler gibberish. After a while, I gave up on my attempt at theological exposition and tried something different: I gave her my phone number.

When the service was over, I bought her a Chinese-English Bible, which she accepted with an enthusiastic smile. And then she did something for which I was utterly unprepared: She started talking. It was not the way she had talked before the service, when, mindful of the people seated around us, we had exchanged only short, quiet sentences. Now her words were coming at me like bullets from a machine gun—and I had no idea what she was saying. Strangely, though, that didn't seem to bother her.

As she went on, I began to feel increasingly uncomfortable. At some point, she was bound to stop talking and expect some kind of response. When that happened, I would likely find it difficult to conceal the fact that I had understood exactly zero percent of what she had been saying, and our relationship might suffer. But when she finished talking, she merely said goodbye and left.

Later that week, she called me. As soon as I said hello, she began talking just as she had at church, stringing her words together so tightly that I couldn't pick a single one out. I was just beginning to wonder if she had some sort of oxygen pump connected to her lungs that enabled her to speak without breathing, when she at last trailed off—and I suddenly realized that it was my turn to say something.

"Uh . . ." I began. I wanted to say "How are you?" but I had the distinct feeling that somewhere in that deluge of words, she had already told me how she was. It was almost certainly too late to ask now. I was in deep linguistic waters without a paddle—or even a boat. Surely she could see that.

As it turned out, "uh" was enough. She picked up again where she had left off, as though I had just agreed with everything she had been saying—which seemed to be all she wanted. And then a minute later, she trailed off again. Once more, I felt obligated to give her a sign that I hadn't died. I was reluctant to test my luck with "uh" again, so I made a concerted effort to ensure that the first sound out of my mouth this time was an actual word, and more importantly, one that would carry information unaltered from my brain to hers. A fitting expression came to mind, and I seized it and ran with it.

"I don't understand," I said.

There was a pause, and I thought that this might be the moment I had been waiting for. She would realize how little I understood, and she would finally give up. But she just went on talking. After another minute or so, I thought that I was able to pick out a phrase that sounded like a conversation closer. The ball was once again in my court.

"Will you go to church again?" I asked.

"Yes," she said, and we both hung up.

On the following Sunday, when I arrived at church, I found her sitting exactly where she had been the week before. She looked up, smiled, and removed her purse from the seat beside her. She was as beautiful as I remembered, but my feelings of attraction were now tempered with dread. It would not do, though, to walk right by her and sit somewhere else while she was smiling and patting the seat next to her.

Halfway through the service, I noticed that Xingmei's leg was touching mine. It wasn't intimate contact by any means—

she was wearing jeans—but I felt as if my entire consciousness now resided in the part of my leg that rested against hers. I also detected a hint of perfume, which I hadn't noticed the previous week, and I wondered idly whether Chinese mothers taught their daughters the art of seduction.

After the service, we parted just as we had before; but this time, I was the one who called her in the middle of the week. It wasn't a well-reasoned decision, but one driven by the memory of her hazel eyes, the feel of her leg against mine, and the scent of her perfume. The phone rang for a while, and then at last someone answered. But it wasn't Xingmei; it was a woman who sounded much older. Her mother, perhaps?

"Is Xingmei there?" I asked shakily in Chinese.

"Who are you?" came the reply.

"I'm her American friend."

There was a pause, and then the woman began talking just as fast as Xingmei always had, but with much greater intensity. I didn't even have a chance to try winning her over with a charming "uh," because she hung up without waiting for a response.

A friend later told me—based on personal experience—that it was common in China for a girl's parents to beat her if she received a phone call from a boy. I hoped that nothing of the sort had happened to Xingmei; but going by the tone of that woman's voice, I wouldn't have been surprised. In any case, I never saw her again, and I had to admit that it was just as well. I would not be able to serve the church effectively if I spent all my energy nursing a questionable relationship with a girl I couldn't even understand.

11

A Lesson in Friendship

It was a cold evening, and Hudson and I were sitting in a dingy little restaurant across the street from Sinopec. For only four kuai—less than fifty cents—we each ordered a steaming bowl of beef noodles and a bottle of beer. Our waiter, a skinny teenage boy, jotted the order down on a well-worn pad of paper.

"Do you want your beer warm or cold?" he asked.

"Cold," I said.

As we waited for our food, we looked around the restaurant at the other patrons, who were watching us with undisguised interest. An elderly couple at the table beside ours had just finished their meal, and as they got up to leave, the husband came over to examine us more closely.

"Father," he said in Chinese, pointing at me. Then his finger swung toward Hudson, and he said, "Son." A broad smile of satisfaction spread across his face, and he nodded, first to himself and then to his wife, proud of his ability to discern biological relationships among foreigners.

I looked at Hudson. His face was as devoid of amusement as mine must have been. He was twenty-two, and I was twenty-three. Did the old man think that I was in my forties, or did he think Hudson was a little boy? Or both? We flashed our teeth at the triumphantly beaming fellow and watched as he and his wife left.

A short time later, our noodles arrived, along with half-liter bottles of beer. Hoping to avoid any further attention, we hunched over our bowls and talked quietly. Our attempt at discretion was futile, however, and we couldn't help but notice an odd-looking pair of guys at another neighboring table who seemed to be arguing about us. One of them was a short, slender fellow with pale skin who appeared to be about eighteen years old. The other looked a little older and was equally short, but with unusually dark complexion and the only afro that I had ever seen on a Chinese person.

The latter seemed especially delighted by our presence. His eyes, wide with wonder, tracked our every move, and he squeaked when he saw me pick up some noodles with my chopsticks. "Oh!" he shouted in English. "You . . . use . . . chopsticks . . . well!" He spoke the words slowly and with a great deal of space between them, as if carefully rehearsing each one in his head before voicing it.

I glanced at Hudson, and he shook his head slightly. He clearly thought it would be best to ignore this strange fellow. I didn't want to be rude, though, so I turned back toward him to acknowledge the compliment.

"Thank you," I said.

This elicited a squeal of delight, and our admirer seemed to take my response as an invitation to engage in further conversation. Our tables were so close that we might as well have been sitting together in the first place, so there was no escaping the series of questions that followed. "Where . . . are . . . you . . . from?" he asked in his exaggeratedly slow manner.

"America," I said.

"OOOHHHHHHHH!"

He asked several more basic questions, and every answer I gave, no matter how mundane, elicited another prolonged "oh" followed by a meaningful glance at his friend. Hudson and I were clearly the most fascinating creatures he had ever encountered. And he was a rather intriguing specimen himself, with his afro and his cartoonish mannerisms. I volleyed most of his questions right back at him.

His name was Hua. I didn't ask his age, but he looked to be pushing thirty. With broken English, he managed to tell me that he was a voice major at the Chinese Conservatory of Music, which was just down the street from Sinopec. This piqued my interest; classical piano was one of my first loves, and after two months in Beijing, I was experiencing withdrawal.

We talked for a few more minutes, and then Hua

indicated that he needed to go. As he and his friend got up to leave, he said that he would be back at the restaurant again on Friday, and he would be delighted if we would be there. My policy at this point was to say yes to anyone and everyone, so I agreed immediately. Then I looked at Hudson.

"It's your date," he said. "I won't be here."

Despite Hua's eccentricities, I felt optimistic about making a new friend. At the very least, it would be an opportunity to practice Chinese. It did occur to me that Hua might be interested in more than a casual friendship—I couldn't be sure, after all, about the exact nature of the delight that glowed in his eyes when he looked at us—but if it came down to that, it would be simple enough to tell him that I wasn't gay. And anyway, since we were both musicians, we might find that we had a lot in common.

On Friday evening, when I walked back into the noodle shop, Hua was sitting at a table for two, waiting. With a broad smile, he beckoned for me to sit down across from him, and we commenced a one-on-one cultural exchange.

Thus far, I had always found it frustrating to communicate with people whose English was as bad as my Chinese; but that wasn't the case with Hua. He was one of the most patient people I'd ever met, and when he spoke in Chinese, he made an effort to pronounce each word slowly and clearly, with as much repetition as I needed. He also exhibited a childlike fascination with every word that I spoke.

In that one meeting, I learned a lot from him. Ningxia, the region where Hua had grown up, was one of the poorest places in China. It was mostly desert, and it was inhabited by the Hui minority, who were categorically Muslim. Hua himself was not Muslim, though. He was an elementary school teacher, and his school had sent him to Beijing to study music. He was subsisting on a stipend of 400 kuai per month—less than fifty dollars.

The question that seemed to interest him most was what I would think of a war between America and China. I had noticed that a lot of young Chinese men wanted to talk about the possibility, as if they felt a collective eagerness to try out their military strength against the infamous Western Bully. I tried parrying Hua's talk of war with fervent wishes that our countries could be friends. He smiled and then pointed at himself.

"Am . . . I . . . your . . . friend?" he asked.

I stared blankly at him for a moment. The question put me in a difficult position. I had just met him, and we could barely communicate with each other. On top of that, he was talking about going to war with my country. Of *course* we weren't friends. And yet, only a petulant elementary school kid would ever say, "You're not my friend."

"Yes," I said.

I wasn't lying; I was being polite. And I expected similar politeness in return—a smile or a nod, or some sort of reciprocal statement, such as, "You're . . . my . . . friend . . . too!" But that wasn't how he responded.

"NO!!!" he shouted. Then, he shook his head in violent slow motion, perfectly matching his speech. "I . . . AM . . .

NOT . . . YOUR . . . FRIEND!"

The shift from the topic of war to that of friendship had given me the impression that we were on our way to making a treaty of sorts; but clearly I had been wrong. The war was still on. I couldn't tell whether he was more offended that I had been so quick to call him a friend or I was more offended by his shouts that we were not friends. Perhaps recognizing that he might have upset me, he rushed to explain that we did not know each other well enough to be friends.

After that, we moved on from the surprisingly hostile topic of friendship to a more harmonious one: music. I told Hua that I played the piano and hoped to see the conservatory. He said that he would be happy to give me a tour and that he was interested in seeing the management institute where I taught; so when we finished eating, I took him across the street to Sinopec.

There really wasn't much for me to show him. Hudson and I were at a very small branch of the school that consisted of a few square, concrete buildings that looked just like any other in China. I took him first to my classroom, and then to my dormitory. His reaction reminded me of what Mark had told me about his Chinese friends' opinion of the "palatial" apartment he had lived in.

"Oh!" he exclaimed. "Your room is so big!"

"Yes," I said. "I am very lucky."

We stared around the room, and I fidgeted as I tried to think of something to say. My eyes landed on my guitar case, and I decided that it might be a good idea to play something.

Just before departing for China, I had learned a song specifically to sing for Chinese friends: "When You Say Nothing at All," by Ronan Keating. I took the guitar out, tuned it, and sang. When I finished, Hua clapped gleefully.

"Very good!" he said in English.

I thanked him and then invited him to sing a song for me in return. It seemed a reasonable request. He was a voice major after all, and he certainly wasn't timid.

"Oh, no!" he said, shaking his head.

The thought of singing for me seemed to mortify him; and I was now out of ideas for what we could do in my dorm, so I put the guitar away and asked him to take me to the conservatory. As we left Sinopec, Hua turned and pointed up at the sign on top of the building.

"You how much money one month?" he asked.

"What?"

"You work. One month. How much money?"

I hesitated. Talking about salary was normal in China—in fact, it was the first question that nearly every taxi driver asked me—but it still made me uncomfortable. However, Hua had already told me how much he was paid, so I figured I might as well tell him.

"2,600 kuai," I said.

It was equivalent to about $313 a month, which I thought was quite modest, even by Chinese standards. I assumed Hua would know that most foreigners earned orders of magnitude more than that, so he should understand that I was far from rich. But when he heard the number, his eyes lit up.

"So much!" he gasped.

When we reached the conservatory, most of the buildings were closed. The muffled sound of scales being played on a piano drifted out of a window. Hua led me to the back of the campus, where there was a soccer field that had a track around it. I had been able to see it from my room at Sinopec, but I hadn't realized that it was part of the music conservatory; for some reason, the idea that musicians might want to play sports was a surprise to me. We walked once around the track, and I decided that it was time to go home.

"We must do this again," I said.

"Oh, yes!" he replied.

Over the next month or so, Hua and I met once or twice a week. We frequented the noodle place and a hole-in-the-wall dumpling joint that made the best boiled dumplings I'd ever had. Sometimes he brought a classmate with him, which was a good thing. None of them spoke any English at all, and their presence forced me to practice my Chinese; plus, having an extra person there always helped us find more pleasant conversation topics than war and friendship.

At one of our meetings, Hua had an announcement to make. "Next . . . week . . . my . . . cousin . . . come . . . from . . . Ningxia," he said. "I . . . want . . . him . . . to . . . meet . . . you."

"That sounds wonderful," I said. "Bring him to my apartment. I will cook American food for you."

"OOH!" he squealed.

And so the following week, I prepared what I considered to be a quintessential American meal: pork chops, corn on the cob, mashed potatoes, and beer. It was nothing fancy, but to my way of thinking, if you wanted to learn about someone's culture, you should go into their home and eat a traditional, home-cooked meal. What better way to introduce Hua and his cousin to America?

I was just mashing the potatoes when they arrived. I opened the door, and Hua was standing there with his cousin, Lang. They could not have looked more different. Whereas Hua was short, shriveled, and dark, with fine curly hair, Lang was tall, muscular, light-skinned, and straight-haired. It seemed impossible that they could be related by blood.

I ushered them to their seats, rushed to finish mashing the potatoes, and then joined them at the table. They waited patiently while I said grace—which was another aspect of their introduction to American culture, as well as a potential step-ping stone toward the Gospel—and I gestured for them to begin eating.

I watched with eager anticipation to see what they would think of the fruit of my labor. I had figured that nothing could be safer than mashed potatoes, but as soon as they spooned a bite into their mouths, their faces paled. They chewed slowly and swallowed with some apparent degree of disgust.

Thinking that perhaps a comment on the cultural signif-icance of the food might take their minds off whatever prob-lems they were having with the taste, I attempted to say in my broken Chinese that mashed potatoes were a very common and traditional American food. Unfortunately, I wasn't sure of the word for "common," so I went with the best approximation I could think of.

"In America, this is a very famous dish," I said.

They exchanged a bug-eyed glance, and Lang burst out laughing. Hua quickly silenced him with a glare and a punch to the shoulder, and then he looked at me apologetically. Lang stared down at his plate, clearly trying to hold in more laughter. Some time passed in silence, and I watched as they took bites of the pork chop and corn before I ventured to speak again.

"Do you believe in God?" I asked.

"No!" Hua exclaimed. This time, he was the one laughing; clearly the notion of believing in God was silly. "I am an atheist," he said slowly in Chinese. I had just learned the word "atheist" from a book called the *Good News Reader*, which was a primer on sharing the Gospel in Chinese. I nodded and then turned to Lang.

"Are you an atheist too?"

To my surprise, Lang shook his head.

"You believe in God?" I asked.

He shook his head again. My unspoken question must have been plain to him, because he answered in a superior tone, "I believe in the True Lord." Again, I understood what he meant because of the *Good News Reader*. The Chinese characters "True Lord" translated to "Allah." So Lang was Muslim.

I looked uncomfortably at the beer in his hand, which I had served him, and then at the half-eaten pork chop on his plate, which he clearly liked more than the mashed potatoes.

Please let him not be violating the tenets of his faith out of mere politeness, I thought.

I cleared my throat nervously. "Is it okay for Muslims to eat pork?"

"No problem," Lang said with a shrug.

"And to drink alcohol?" I asked, pointing at his beer.

"Beer is not alcohol!" he said. Then he barked a laugh and glanced at Hua again as if I had just made the stupidest suggestion he'd ever heard. I looked from his laughing face to the beer and wondered just how much alcohol a beverage had to contain in order to qualify as alcohol. I also wondered how he would respond if I told him he wasn't a real Muslim. I wouldn't have minded offending him after the way he'd laughed at my mashed potatoes; but I was determined to remain gracious.

We continued eating, and after a while, Hua spoke up again.

"Do you have sugar?" he asked.

"Yes."

I found a bag of sugar in a cabinet and handed it to him, wondering what he intended to do with it. He looked at the bag and frowned.

"Do you have *red* sugar?" He asked.

I guessed that he meant brown sugar, and I found some for him. Then I watched as he dumped a heaping spoonful of it onto the half-cup of mashed potatoes that remained on his plate. And then another spoonful. And another. When there was as much sugar as mashed potatoes on his plate, he began stirring. Then, gingerly, he tasted the mixture.

"Much better," he declared in Chinese. He then handed the bag of brown sugar to Lang, who mixed the rest of it into his mashed potatoes, and they proceeded to clean their plates.

When we parted that evening, Hua declared that he would be cooking for me the next time we met. It was time, he had decided, for me to see his apartment. That he even lived in an apartment was a surprise to me, since I had assumed that he must be staying in a dormitory on the conservatory campus. I responded as I always did—by accepting the invitation.

As our next meeting approached, I worried that Hua might want to treat me to some Chinese delicacy that would be as repulsive to me as my potatoes had apparently been to him. And so it was with more than a little trepidation that I biked to his apartment complex, climbed the stairs to his unit, and knocked on his door at the agreed-upon time.

Hua opened the door, and I saw four other people—three boys and a girl, all of about college age—crowding around behind him to get a look at me. He had to push them back to make room for me to enter, and he introduced them to me as his roommates. I glanced at the girl. *A female roommate?* I thought. *They're probably having sex.*

After the introductions, Hua gave me a tour. The whole place could almost have fit into my one-room apartment at Sinopec. Each room was lit by a bare light bulb in the middle of the ceiling. The floors were concrete, and the walls and ceilings were plaster. Everywhere I looked, the plaster was peeling off. The beds were mere pallets on the floor.

Dinner was cooking in a pot on an electric hot plate at the center of the table, which was sized to seat four people. Hua lifted the lid on the pot to show me what was in it, and I saw noodles, bok choy, and mushrooms, as well as the ubiquitous "wood ear" fungus.

"I think it's done," he said.

He ushered me onto one of six three-legged stools that were crammed tightly around the table, and the others took their seats as well. Hua ladled the noodles and broth into a bowl for each person, and after a minute everyone was slurping away noisily. Then, halfway through the meal, the front door opened, and another boy entered.

"Our sixth roommate," Hua said to me.

I recognized the newcomer as the short, skinny, pale guy who had been with Hua at the noodle restaurant when we first met. He strutted across the room like a model on a runway, and his roommates gasped collectively, staring at his legs.

"You bought new pants!" one of them exclaimed.

"Yes," he said.

I looked closely at his pants and saw that they did indeed look new—and shiny. They were blue jeans, perfectly creased, turned up about four inches at the cuffs, with an iridescent lavender thread worked into the weave. The fabric shimmered as he turned. Ooh's and ah's echoed around the room, and the sixth roommate's face glowed with pride. Until that moment, I had never imagined that the expression "Mr. Fancy Pants" might have occasion to be used literally.

"How much did they cost?" asked another roommate.

"More than a hundred," Fancy Pants replied. His voice exuded a smug pride—not for having gotten a good deal, but for having spent a large sum. It amounted to thirteen or fourteen dollars, but in China that was a huge amount to pay for a pair of pants. He strutted around for another minute or so, collecting further admiration, and then he disappeared into one of the bedrooms.

"What are you doing?" Hua shouted after him. "Come eat!"

"Let me change first," came the reply. Apparently, Fancy Pants didn't want to risk spilling food on his expensive new threads.

When I had stayed long enough not to be thought rude, I announced that I had to leave. The conversation had been awkward, and I had the impression that Hua's roommates would be relieved to see me go. Hua accompanied me down the stairs and out into the crisp night air—where I discovered that my bike was missing.

I walked home feeling dejected, not just because my bike had been stolen, but because I saw that I was failing to connect with Hua or his roommates. I had come to China with the romantic notion that I could make friends with people of any background; but the sad truth—that building genuine friendships across linguistic and cultural barriers was *hard*—was just now beginning to sink in.

12

A Solemn Vow

When the fit of vomiting was over at last, I wiped my mouth with a wad of toilet paper and leaned back, panting, against the bathroom wall. I knew perfectly well what the cause of my suffering was, and it had nothing to do with spoiled food. I'd had too much to drink, plain and simple.

Perhaps I was getting no more than I deserved, but I felt betrayed nonetheless—not by my students, but by my own body. If the damn thing had thought to give me a sign that I was going too far, I would have stopped earlier. But no, it had pretended all evening that it was fine, and now I was in agony.

It was a weekday, shortly before Christmas, but that hadn't been the occasion for celebration. The youngest student in our class—Michael, who was a mere twenty-six years old—had just gotten married. So Hudson and I had found ourselves in a private dining room at a nearby restaurant, sitting with all fifteen of our students around two large, circular tables. Justin, the prince of mischief, had been seated on my left.

"Would you like some white wine?" he asked.

I hesitated. Before going to China, I had probably had a total of ten beers, ten glasses of wine, and five margaritas. This was partly because I didn't care for the taste of alcohol, and partly because of my religious convictions. But I hadn't seen much wine at all since coming to China, and I thought that a glass of white wine would be nice. So I said yes.

When I saw what Justin poured into my glass, though, I groaned. It wasn't wine at all, but *baijiu*—the quintessential alcoholic beverage of China. The name literally means "white alcohol"—hence the mistranslation—and with an alcohol content anywhere between thirty and fifty percent, it's more like vodka than anything else.

Justin probably would have filled my glass to the top, but Frank, the student on my right, stopped him before it was even halfway full. Justin argued with Frank for a while, but he caved in after a minute, likely because Frank was older, and moved on to fill the others' glasses.

"Don't drink too much," Frank said to me quietly, his eyes filled with concern.

Soon everyone else's glass was full, and after a moment we were all standing, holding our glasses in the air. "Lai, lai, lai," the students yelled. *Come, come, come. It is time to drink.*

A toast was made in honor of Michael, who was standing sheepishly in the middle of the room, and then we raised our glasses to our lips.

I took only the smallest of sips, but even so it was like swallowing a glowing coal. The vile fluid burned my esophagus all the way down, before turning my stomach into a furnace. At the same time, the vapors made their way up into my nose, and my eyes began to water. Justin watched with a broad grin, seeming on the verge of erupting in a fit of sadistic giggles.

For the rest of the evening, between bites of food, one student or another wanted to drink with me. They clinked glasses with me, careful to keep theirs below mine as a show of respect for their teacher, and urged me to take big gulps. I knew I wouldn't be able to handle much, though, so I limited myself to sips, and I sat back and watched as my students began to shed their usual restraint.

The sheer amount that they drank surprised me. My Asian friends in college all had a low alcohol tolerance, and I had somehow gotten the impression that Chinese people didn't drink much. But as the celebration of Michael's wedding unfolded, I discovered that nothing could be further from the truth. No one drank more than Michael, and within half an hour, he was stumbling around, red-faced, slurring his speech.

I, on the other hand, was doing quite well. I finished my half-glass in tiny sips over a period of about an hour, and I didn't feel much of an effect at all. So when Justin poured me another half-glass, I just kept sipping at it gradually. I assumed that if I went slowly enough, I wouldn't get drunk—and it seemed that I was right. Another two hours passed, and I only felt a little tipsy.

When the party was over and we had all taken taxis back to Sinopec, I went to bed feeling fine. But some time after midnight, I woke suddenly, overcome by nausea, rolled out of bed, stumbled into the bathroom, and proceeded to retch up the exquisite delicacies I had consumed at the banquet. Some ten minutes later, when I collapsed onto my bed once more, I felt overwhelmingly relieved.

Thank God that's over, I thought.

But it turned out not to be over at all. More fits followed, every hour, like clockwork. After each bout, I drank a glass of water, hoping to dilute the poison that remained within me, to speed its passage. The night dragged on like none I'd ever experienced; and yet somehow, before I knew it, I was awakened by the intrusion of daylight and the ring of my alarm clock.

It was time to go to class.

Still feeling miserable, I made my way to the classroom and slogged through the day's lesson, all the while worrying that I would vomit in front of my students. If that happened, what would they think? All of them were there except for Michael, and they seemed perfectly fine. That only worsened my mood; they were the ones who had put me in this situation, and they hadn't suffered at all.

It wasn't until I was walking back to my room at the end

of the day that I noticed a dull pain in my right side, just below my ribs. I tried to ignore it, but it lingered over the next two or three days, and I grew increasingly certain that it was my liver, inflamed from too much alcohol. The longer the pain persisted, the more worried I became. I was just beginning to think about looking for a doctor when it finally began to fade.

I felt as if God had granted me a second chance at life.

"I will never drink *baijiu* again," I vowed, looking into the mirror. I was talking to both God and myself. I had always believed that it was a sin to get drunk, but I now knew firsthand just how unpleasant the physical consequences could be. Never wanting to experience them again, I prayed that God would help me keep my new vow. I saw no reason why he wouldn't.

A few weeks later, the fall semester came to an end. The occasion was marked by a commencement ceremony, at which I made a speech stressing that in addition to "graduation," the word "commencement" also meant "the beginning of something new." I expressed my hope that the students' completion of our English course marked not an end, but a beginning of new friendships and new opportunities for them. It was a beautiful idea; I had lifted it from the speech that was made at my own college graduation.

After the ceremony, one of the students pulled me aside. He was beaming. "Now I know that my English really did improve during the semester! At the opening ceremony, I didn't understand anything you said. But just now, I understood your whole speech!"

That night, the students took us out for one last celebration. Their studies at the management institute had come to an end, and we would likely never see most of them again. So once more, we piled into taxis and went to a restaurant with a private dining room. As we were walking into the restaurant, Justin fell into step beside me.

"You have to drink more than you did last time," he said.

"What?"

"You didn't drink enough last time," he said. "And anyway, every time you go out, you have to try to drink more than the last time."

"You think I didn't drink enough last time?" I asked in disbelief. "I vomited all night!"

"We *all* vomited all night!" Justin shot back.

I keenly remembered my vow not to drink *baijiu* again, and as we found our seats, I tried to explain it to Justin. I told him that I just didn't have the habit of drinking. I wanted to respect all of the students and be their friend, but I just couldn't handle *baijiu*. Justin stared back at me, processing my words slowly. "Okay," he said at last. "You just drink beer, then. The rest of us will drink *baijiu*."

The banquet was every bit as raucous as Michael's wedding celebration, and several students pressured me to drink in greater volume when they noticed I was just having beer. I only saw one way out, and I took it: I pretended to get drunk. It wasn't hard. All I had to do was act like my students, and since they really *were* drunk, they wouldn't be able to tell the difference. For all I knew, some of them might have been pretending for the same reason.

It worked. When the evening was over, two very concerned-looking students escorted me back to my room to make sure I got there safely. They only left when they were convinced that I wasn't going to pass out and die, and when I closed the door behind them, I breathed an enormous sigh of relief. I had been deceitful, but at least I had been able to keep my vow.

Days later, when the last of my students had left Beijing to return home, the memory of being pressured to drink was not what stayed with me. Instead, it was their kindness and hospitality—the way Jian had taken me shopping to ensure that I had everything I wanted; the way Justin had begun consulting with his wife about finding a suitable woman for me; and the way all of them had come to visit me in my room, bearing gifts, when I had been out with a fever. I still had another semester to go with ESI, but I had already decided that one year would not be enough.

In addition to thinking about the impact my students had had on me, I wondered how much of an effect I'd had on them. My main purpose was to win souls for Christ, and throughout the semester, I had prayed daily for every student by name. I had even talked to a few of them about God, but none seemed interested. Perhaps I shouldn't have been surprised—after all, I had prayed for many friends throughout college with only negative results—but still, I was eager to see God do his mighty work, and a part of me was wondering why my prayers went unanswered.

The obvious reason was that he wasn't there. But that wasn't the answer I wanted, and it was easy to think of other possible explanations. To the Lord, the scriptures say, a thousand years are like a day. I knew that the seeds I was sowing today might not bear fruit for generations to come, and I had to be okay with that. It was not my place to demand to see the fruit of my labor; my only task was to plant the seeds of the Gospel in faith, and that was something I was determined to continue doing.

13

Fireworks in the Distance

It wasn't so much the shaking of the bed that had disturbed my sleep—one gets used to that on an overnight train—but the sound of distant, muffled booms. A look through the window at first revealed nothing but pitch blackness blanketing the countryside. Then, off in the distance, an expanding sphere of red sparks blossomed just above the horizon. A moment later, there was another, and then another. Soon, everywhere I looked, bursts of colored light were blooming and fading.

I checked my watch. It was just after midnight. The new year—Spring Festival—had officially arrived, and the whole nation was celebrating. Even deep in the countryside where I was now, every household was setting off as many fireworks as they had been able to afford. Most of the displays were far enough away that they were silent to my ears, as if happening in a separate world, one altogether inaccessible to me.

I was on my way to a city called Yangzhou to visit one of my students, a man in his late forties named Sun. The only train tickets available had been for New Year's Eve, and that was a shame because it meant that I had to miss the celebration that was going on all across the country at the moment. There was an upside, though: Had I gotten the tickets I wanted, I'd have been crammed into the train car with dozens of others, likely forced to stand throughout the twelve-hour ride; but as it was, I had the car entirely to myself.

The sound of fireworks continued throughout the night, and in the morning, as the train snaked its way into Yangzhou, the cacophony grew louder, in part because the population was denser, but also because people were jumping out of bed to set off more fireworks upon awakening—if they had even slept at all. The intensity of it didn't really hit me until I stepped off the train. The rapid-fire pops from strings of firecrackers, exploding near and far in all directions, added up to a deafening, almost-white noise. It was all I could focus on when Sun, together with his wife, Elaine, and their college-aged son, Bo, found me and ushered me into a taxi.

They took me first to my hotel, where I checked in and we all ate breakfast together, and then to their home. It was a typical Chinese condo, a small unit in a large, concrete-and-brick complex, with two bedrooms, a living room, a kitchen, and a single bathroom. Elaine went immediately to the stereo to put on some English music, while Sun and Bo set up a gold-filigreed game board, behind which they ushered me to sit down. Evidently, my first activity of the new year would be to face Bo in a game of Chinese chess.

I should have lost, but Sun's sense of hospitality would never allow it. With silent gestures—because he still couldn't speak more than a few words of English, even after a semester in my class—Sun dictated my every move. And in between my own moves, I witnessed the full range of fatherly emotions, from pride to despair, as Sun reacted to each of his son's decisions. After only a few minutes, Bo was shaking my hand, and Sun was clapping me on the back to congratulate me on a well-deserved win. Then the board was reset, and we played again. I bested Bo three or four times in this manner before it was decided that we should move on to something else.

"Do you like Chinese music?" Elaine asked.

I said that I did, and she disappeared for a moment before returning with a *guzheng*, a traditional Chinese stringed instrument. She played a few pieces for me, and when she began telling me about the history of the instrument, I suddenly realized that her English was remarkably better than her husband's. I decided to ask her where she had learned it.

"I had an American teacher in college," she said.

I thought for a moment. Judging by Elaine's age, that would have been in the early nineteen eighties—just a few years after China opened up to the West. I knew that then, just as now, many of the foreigners who came to teach English in China were missionaries in disguise, and I wondered whether her teacher might have shared the Gospel with her—and whether any seeds that had been sewn all those years ago might be ready to yield a harvest now.

"She gave me a Bible," Elaine said.

I stared back at her in shock. It was as if she had read the question in my mind, as if the Holy Spirit were prompting her, nudging her toward salvation. Thinking that perhaps this was why God had brought me to Yangzhou, I opened my mouth to pursue the subject further, but before I could even get a word out, she had pulled open a drawer and begun rummaging through it. "I still have it," she said, and a moment later, she was holding it out reverently for me to see.

"Did you read it?" I asked.

"I tried," she said. "But it was too difficult to understand."

In my mind, I whispered a prayer of thanksgiving. During the preceding days, I had been reviewing the *Good News Reader,* in which one of the lessons was about how to describe the contents of the Bible in Chinese. I had been preparing for just such a moment as this. Resolved to help Elaine understand the Bible in her own language, I began to recite the sentences I had learned in that lesson.

"The Bible has sixty-six small books," I began.

It was an easy sentence. I knew all of the words perfectly well: Bible, has, sixty-six, small, and book. But it turned out there was a problem I could not have foreseen. When you put the words "small" and "book" together, it sounds like you're *trying* to say the word for "novel," which is actually composed of the words "small" and "speak." This proved to be an issue for Elaine.

"I think you mean sixty-six novels," she said.

"No," I said. "They're not novels. They're small books."

Bo was now standing beside me, looking on as I held the Bible open to the table of contents page. I was planning to describe the Old and New Testaments and discuss what the different books were about—history, prophecy, poetry, and letters—and now I had not just one listener, but two. I decided to start over.

"The Bible has sixty-six small books," I repeated.

This time, it was Bo who objected. "Surely you mean novels," he said. "'Small books' is not a word in Chinese."

I frowned. The *Good News Reader* was supposed to have been written by a native Chinese speaker, but it was clearly failing me nonetheless. So I switched to English and proceeded with my little presentation, closing with a simple summary of the Gospel. As I listened to the words coming out of my own mouth, I began to sense that very little about the Bible sounded appealing to people who hadn't grown up learning about it. The bored look in their eyes confirmed this; and as soon as I had finished, Elaine declared that it was time for dinner.

The next morning, Bo came to my hotel room to pick me up. It turned out that the plan was for me to spend the whole day with him. And the next day. And the day after that. It took me a while to realize that this was the real reason Sun had invited me to spend the holiday with his family in the first place—to give his son a chance to practice his English with a foreigner. Such opportunities were rare, and Sun considered it well worth financing my vacation.

It wasn't until the fourth day that we deviated from this pattern. That morning, Bo took me back to his parents' house, in front of which was a car that hadn't been there before. Sun and Elaine were loading it with boxes of fruit, *baijiu*, and tea, and Sun announced that he would be driving us to Elaine's brother's home. "Where did you get the car?" I asked as I helped him with a box.

"I borrow," Sun said.

"I didn't know you had a driver's license," I said.

He laughed.

Elaine's brother, Hui, lived in the town of Dongtai, about two hours northeast of Yangzhou, where he operated a tea shop. When we arrived at his home, Sun proudly introduced me to Hui's family, which was quite large. I was the first foreigner that most of them had met, and my presence seemed to be the highlight of the day. Pleasantries were exchanged, and then the women retreated to the kitchen, while the men commenced smoking and drinking in the living room.

During one lull in the conversation, Hui looked from me to his eight-year-old son, Bing, and said to him, "Why don't you play chess with our foreign friend?" Everyone in the room—except for Bing and myself—murmured agreement with what a wonderful idea this was. Moments later, Bing and I were looking at each other over yet another gold-filigreed chess set.

"You go first," Hui said to me.

I pushed a pawn—or "foot soldier," as the piece was called in Chinese—forward. Another murmur passed through the room as the adults discussed the wisdom, or perhaps idiocy, of my opening move. There shouldn't have been much for them to say, though; moving a central pawn forward is, I believe, as common an opening in Chinese chess as it is in international chess. And then Hui barked.

"You know how to respond to that!" he said.

It was clear from the start that Hui lacked the sense of hospitality Sun had shown during my earlier games with Bo. I was on my own, and it took an embarrassingly short time for me to be slaughtered. When it was over, Bing looked more relieved than happy to have won, and I found myself wondering whether Hui would have punished him for losing.

The men continued talking and drinking until one of the women entered to announce that the food was ready, at which point they gathered around the dining table and sat down. I was ushered to the position of honor, just beside Hui, with Bo on my other side so that he could translate for me. I noticed that once the men had all sat down, there were no empty seats left—and the women had not come in yet.

"What about your mom and the other ladies?" I whispered to Bo.

"They will serve us the food and then eat when we are done," he replied.

Alcohol was poured all around, even though most of the men were already red-faced. I insisted on just having beer, not *baijiu*. Hui seemed on the verge of insisting that I take some *baijiu*, but Sun came to my rescue and poured me a small glass of beer, for which I was extremely grateful. At least I would have no trouble keeping my vow.

A toast was made—to me, to the family, to health, and to various other things that I didn't quite make out—and then the women began to serve us. Even as we ate, they worked in the kitchen to prepare more food. I could hear the almost frantic sound of knives clacking against wooden boards, and vegetables sizzling in a wok.

One of the first things set on the table was a large glass bowl full of shrimp that were swimming around. I found it a bit strange. Was it an aesthetic thing, I wondered? An aquarium of sorts, for us to watch as we ate?

"What's that for?" I asked.

"They're shrimp," Bo said. "You eat them."

And sure enough, everyone started reaching in with their chopsticks, catching shrimp in mid-swim, putting them in their mouths, chewing, and swallowing. Hui grabbed one with his chopsticks and placed it on my plate. It lay there, twitching feebly.

Slowly, not wanting to offend my host, I picked up the shrimp with my chopsticks and ate it, crunching down queasily on its exoskeleton, its legs, its head, and its antennae. Its insides oozed out into my mouth like jelly, and it proved to be every bit as disgusting as I had imagined. It took some effort to swallow, and once I had done so I saw that everyone was smiling at me in approval.

"Now you need to drink *baijiu*," Bo said.

I blinked at him. "Why?"

"If you eat live shrimp without drinking *baijiu*, you will get food poisoning."

As I took in the matter-of-fact expression on Bo's face, anger welled up within me, and I felt my hatred for China's alcohol culture begin to solidify. *Baijiu* was an awful-tasting concoction anyway, and the only reason people drank it was to get drunk—or, evidently, to fend off food poisoning. As it happened, I'd just had a case of food poisoning a week earlier, and it had been decidedly worse than the illness I'd suffered after drinking too much at Michael's wedding celebration. With that in mind, I accepted a glass of *baijiu* from Hui and drank it—telling myself once again that this was the last time.

The rest of the meal passed in a sort of haze. When the men had finished eating, the women cleared away the dirty dishes and then sat on stools in the kitchen to eat the leftovers. The men, meanwhile, exhausted from the labor of feasting, leaned back in their chairs at the dinner table and puffed away at cigarettes while talking about politics—a conversation in which I had no hope of participating.

I was relieved when it was time to go, but the day was far from over. We had another banquet to attend in Nanjing, a nearby city where Sun's younger brother lived. So we bid farewell to Hui and his family and set off on the three-hour drive for Nanjing. I noted that Sun's driving was comparable to that of a typical Chinese taxi driver—which is to say that he always wanted to drive faster than everyone else on the road and swerved around a lot as he passed other cars—and I tried not to think about how much *baijiu* he had just consumed.

When we reached Nanjing, Bo explained to me that his uncle—Sun's little brother—was an officer in the People's Liberation Army and would be hosting us for dinner at the army base.

"What's his rank?" I asked.

"Some kind of general," Bo said.

A short time later, Sun turned the car onto a drive that brought us to a security checkpoint. Two guards emerged from a guardhouse, and one of them spoke to Sun while the other walked around the car, looking inside. He examined me through the window for a while as Sun answered questions that the other guard was asking. Bo translated certain parts for me.

"Foreigners are not allowed to enter the base," he said.

"What am I supposed to do, then?" I asked. I felt a little peeved that they hadn't considered this issue earlier, and I was beginning to worry that my presence might ruin everybody's evening. Perhaps Sun would send me with Bo to eat dinner on our own somewhere while the rest of the family enjoyed the banquet at the base. That would have been fine with me.

"Don't worry," Bo said.

Some phone calls were made, and the guards at last opened the gate to let us through, with an admonition that I was not allowed to take any pictures. We drove deeper into the base and parked, and Sun led us into a building, where we entered a small banquet hall about the size of a tennis court. Once inside, we were met by Sun's brother—the General.

I had been expecting him to be in uniform, but he was wearing an ordinary, gray Western suit. He didn't look much like Sun, I thought. His face was flabbier, and he had gray in his hair. I stood there for a minute with Bo beside me while Sun spoke to his brother, gesturing toward me and laughing.

"My father is telling him about you," Bo said.

When Sun finally finished talking, the General turned toward me. I was ready to shake hands, but he didn't seem interested in touching me. Instead, he issued what sounded like a cross between a bark and a cough, and then he cleared his throat. As far as I could tell, he had not actually spoken any words. I looked at Bo questioningly.

"Of course, you know what that means," Bo said.

"Actually, no," I said. "I didn't understand."

"He said 'Welcome!'"

"Oh."

I bowed slightly to the General and thanked him for his hospitality. After several more introductions were made—there were about thirty people in all—it was time for the meal to begin, and we all gathered around the enormous, round banquet table. Drinks were poured, and I was asked whether I wanted *baijiu*.

"No," I said. "No alcohol, please."

No one seemed inclined to pressure me, for which I was grateful. Here, at least, keeping my vow wouldn't be an issue. When the General saw that all of the drinks had been poured, he stood up and began making a speech. At one point, he gestured toward me, and everyone's eyes fell on me. Bo leaned over to translate.

"My uncle says that no foreigner has ever before been allowed to enter this base," he said. "Today he is making the first exception to this rule for you since you are my father's teacher."

I was just beginning to feel honored, when Bo leaned toward me again and translated the next sentence. "My uncle says that since he is honoring you in this way, you must drink with him."

I looked at the General. He was smiling at me, a politician's smile, holding a full glass of *baijiu* up in the air. One of the adults beside me pushed an equally full glass into my hand. I looked uneasily from the glass to the General and frowned, thinking once again about my vow.

"I suggest you drink," said Bo.

I drank, and as I did so, I saw the situation for what it was. The General wasn't honoring me at all. At that moment, I was his puppet, and he was manipulating me in front of his family in a petty display of power. After I had complied, he ignored me, and I spent the rest of the evening chatting with Bo when his relatives weren't shouting at him across the table to ask how he was progressing in school.

When the meal was over an hour later, I was eager to get back to my hotel room and be alone. Sun, red-faced with inebriation, led us back to his borrowed car. I had been forced to do enough things against my will already that day, and I finally worked up the nerve to speak up about something that was bothering me. "I don't mean to offend you," I said, "but

I really don't feel comfortable riding with you after you've had so much alcohol."

"Don't worry," Sun said. "I'm a good driver."

"Go on," Bo said. "Get in."

I hesitated for a moment. What other option did I have? I didn't want to think about what might happen if I walked away from Sun on the grounds of an army base where I wasn't even technically allowed to be. So I got in the car. In short order, Sun was once again speeding along the highway, swerving around every car we encountered. He was putting my life—and the lives of his whole family—at risk, and he thought nothing of it.

I was all too aware that China had a much higher rate of fatal traffic accidents than just about any other country, and as I watched the road in terror, I decided that Chinese drivers needed to be educated, both about safe driving habits and about the dangers of drinking and driving. I spent two hours entertaining a detailed fantasy about opening a chain of driving schools across the country, and when we arrived back in Yangzhou at last and they dropped me off at my hotel, I felt like kissing the ground.

Two days later, I was bidding Sun and Elaine farewell before boarding a train for Beijing. The last thing they said to me was that they now wanted me to call them *Gan Ba* and *Gan Ma*—relatively intimate forms of address reserved for elders whom you regard like a father and mother. It was touching, and I complied; but at the same time, I found myself thinking that after spending a week with them, they seemed not closer, but more unreachable than ever, like fireworks in the distance.

14

A Shady Offer

Two weeks into the spring semester at Sinopec, everything seemed to be going well. Hudson and I were in the middle of our unit on baseball, and I had just finished showing the students *The Rookie*, a film about a middle-aged high school teacher whose life and family nearly fall apart as he pursues his dream of becoming a big-league pitcher. The previous group of students had loved it, and I assumed that this group would as well. But as soon as it was over, the class monitor, Mike, pulled me aside.

"Mr. Rambow, we need to talk about the movie," he said.

"What about it?" I asked.

"It's not appropriate to show in China."

I stared at Mike in shock. *Not appropriate*? It was about

as innocent as any movie I knew of. There was no dirty language, no sex, no violence, no drugs—nothing I could think of that would justify calling it "inappropriate." I asked him what was wrong with it.

"It encourages people to abandon their responsibilities and pursue selfish dreams," he said. "The character in the movie should have stayed home and taken care of his family. Leaving family to pursue a dream is not what good people do. You should not show us movies with such themes."

I didn't know what to say. In America, almost from birth, I had been hammered by the "pursue your dream" message. I was accustomed to an environment in which kids were encouraged to aspire to be artists, actors, athletes—whatever they wanted to be. It had never occurred to me that someone might find such a way of thinking to be inappropriate. Surely Mike's concern was ridiculous, I thought. And yet . . . I could see his point. What kind of society would we have if *everyone* left their family to pursue a dream?

"Check with me next time before you show us a movie," Mike said.

This confirmed my suspicion that a "class monitor" was more than just a teacher's assistant, and from then on, I worried about what Mike was thinking of our lessons and what he might be telling the administrators. Would there be trouble when we arrived at our unit on religion? I tried to lay down my fears and put my trust in God, but I knew full well that God allowed some missionaries to be kicked out of the country—or worse. I couldn't take it for granted that things would go as smoothly as they had the previous semester.

At least one thing hadn't changed, however: Our students still vied for opportunities to take Hudson and me out to dinner. There was one in particular who seemed determined to ingratiate himself with us: Gabe. He was a short, slim businessman in his early forties with glasses and dark, wavy hair. Whenever he talked to me, his left eye would remain fixed on me while his right eye drifted off to the side as if searching for something more stimulating than our conversation.

"Have you eaten dog?" Gabe asked me one day.

"No," I answered without thinking.

"Then I will take you to eat dog!"

A few nights later, we found ourselves going out with Gabe and a large group of students to a Miao restaurant. The Miao are a Chinese minority—one of the 55 officially recognized groups—and they are known for eating dog meat, among other things. As always, we were seated in a private dining room around a large, round banquet table. The waiters were all supposed to belong to the Miao minority, and they were dressed in colorful, beaded and embroidered clothing in the Miao style. Once they had served us our food, they gathered around the table and sang a traditional Miao song for us. Then it was time to eat.

I had been expecting them to put an entire roasted dog on a big platter in the middle of the table, as I had seen done with goats. But as it turned out, the dish that contained dog meat was just one of many other dishes on the table, and it was rather inconspicuous. Under Gabe's watchful eye, I tried a few bites. It was smothered in such a potent spicy sauce that I couldn't have said much about the flavor of the meat itself. It might as well have been goat for all I knew.

Bottles of beer and *baijiu* were opened, and I insisted on having only beer, much to Gabe's amusement. Beer was a girl's drink, after all. Gabe ostentatiously downed quite a bit of *baijiu*, and he appeared to get drunk rather quickly—though maybe his lazy eye was just playing tricks on me as it rolled about in that disturbing manner. At one point, I was coming out of the restroom just as Gabe was on his way in, and he stopped me.

"After dinner, I will take you to sing ka-la-O-K," he said.

I recognized the Chinese pronunciation of "karaoke." I had no interest in it whatsoever, but I was still in the habit of going along with whatever my hosts wanted to do. So I said I would be happy to go. He looked delighted. "Yes," he said. "We will sing ka-la-O-K, and I will get some girls for you and Hudson!"

I wasn't sure what he meant by that last part. After staring at him in confusion for a moment, I decided that he was planning to introduce us to a couple of girls he knew and take us all to a coffee shop—a blind date of sorts. That was the only image my feeble imagination was capable of conjuring, and it was what I had in mind when I told Gabe that it sounded like fun. Looking happy, he went into the restroom, and I returned to the table.

"Gabe wants to take us to sing karaoke," I told Hudson when I sat back down. "He said he's going to get us some girls."

"What?" Hudson asked. He was probably wondering whether he had heard me right. It was rather loud, with several of the men laughing raucously.

"Just now, when I came out of the bathroom, he said he was going to get some girls for us and take us to sing karaoke," I explained, still imagining a blind double-date at a coffee shop—which didn't even make sense because coffee shops weren't yet a thing in China. Then, stupidly, I added, "Gabe's the man!"

Hudson shook his head. "I don't think it's a good idea," he said.

"Nonsense—it'll be fun!" I replied.

Another hour or so passed, and the eating and drinking wound down. We walked out of the restaurant, and most of the students took taxis back to Sinopec, leaving Hudson and me standing at the curb with Gabe and two other students, Evan and Jeff. Jeff was red-faced and tipsy, while Evan stood, clear-eyed and stoic, with a faint smile on his lips.

"Hollywood?" Gabe asked them.

Evan nodded, and Jeff barked something in Chinese with drunken enthusiasm. Seconds later, Gabe had hailed cabs for us, and Hudson and I climbed into one with him, while Evan and Jeff got in the other. We drove for a while, coming at last to an unfamiliar part of town that had lots of trees—I wasn't even sure we were *in* town anymore—and after we rounded a bend, a building with flashing neon lights came into view. It said, "Hollywood."

We stepped out of our taxis and entered the building,

where a hostess ushered us through a maze of hallways into a private room that had a big, U-shaped couch facing a television and a large tea table in the middle. At a gesture from Gabe, we sat down on the couch and waited. A minute passed, and then about seven or eight girls walked into the room and lined up in front of us. They were all young and pretty, ranging from perhaps eighteen to twenty-five in age.

"Choose one," Gabe said.

"Uh . . ." I stuttered. It was just now dawning on me how woefully inaccurate my vision of chatting with girls in a coffee shop had been. This was no casual blind date. Rather, Gabe was intending to pay for escorts for us—girls to keep us company while we sang karaoke, and to do much more than that when we'd had our fill of singing.

"I told you this was a bad idea," Hudson said.

Everyone was staring at us. Evan, as usual, had that faint enigmatic grin on his face, while Jeff seemed about to burst into laughter. The girls were appraising us as openly as they expected us to appraise them, and Gabe was beginning to look worried. "If you don't like any of them, tell me. They will bring another set," he said.

"Let's just choose some that are decently clothed and get out of here as soon as we can," Hudson whispered. "And how about if we choose for each other?" he added.

I wasn't sure what Hudson's reasoning was, but his suggestion seemed like a good idea—as if it would somehow remove us a step from the act of choosing prostitutes for ourselves. I nodded and then looked at the girls again. In the middle was one who had an innocent, girl-next-door look. Not at all naughty. She was wearing a burgundy blouse. I decided to pick her for Hudson.

"The girl in the red shirt," I said, pointing at her.

She started to walk toward me, but then I pointed toward Hudson. She looked from me to Hudson, and a murmur passed around the room as she went to sit beside him. It was now Hudson's turn, and he pointed to a tall girl in a dark blue dress, with big, dark eyes and long, shiny black hair. I thought that she was the most beautiful one in the lineup, and I was secretly delighted that he had chosen her. Having picked up on our system, the girl sat next to me and, smiling, took my hand in hers.

Gabe, Evan, and Jeff then chose girls for themselves, at one point asking for a different batch to be brought in. When the selection was over, drinks and snacks were ordered—bottles of beer and *baijiu*, for everyone to share, along with bowls of peanuts and sunflower seeds. Then the karaoke machine was turned on, and our students settled their escorts comfortably on their laps while Hudson and I sat awkwardly beside ours, wondering how it was all going to end.

It was perhaps an hour or two later when Hudson and I were back at Sinopec, conducting something of a debriefing. What, if anything, were we to do about this experience, this side of China that we had not planned to see? From our reading, we had "known" already that lots of girls came from the countryside and ended up working in such places, but it wasn't until now that the knowledge had been driven home.

We talked about the girls, and we prayed for them, asking that God would free them from their circumstances. And then we went to bed. While I waited for sleep to come, I thought about the one thing that I'd kept secret from Hudson: the business card that I'd left in the brothel. Would that beautiful, dark-eyed girl in the blue dress, whose name I had never learned, take me up on my offer to bring her to church? And what were my own motives, really?

About a week later, at around ten o'clock at night, there was a knock on my dormitory door. I was expecting to find Hudson there, but when I opened the door, I saw that it was Gabe, with Evan standing by his side. Without invitation, Gabe stumbled inside, clearly drunk. Evan followed him in reluctantly. He, at least, had the grace to look slightly apologetic for disturbing me.

Without a word, Gabe took a chair in my tiny living room and lit a cigarette. I frowned, but he didn't notice. Evan did, though, and he tried to get Gabe to put out his cigarette. They argued softly for a moment, and Gabe apparently won, because he kept smoking and Evan stopped talking. Then Gabe turned to me, with a disturbingly serious look in his eyes.

"I'm going to work in Houston in the future," he said.

"That's great," I said.

Gabe knew, of course, that I was from Houston. It made sense that he might want to ask me about it. It wasn't the ideal time to talk, but I supposed I could recommend some tourist attractions and local restaurants. I started thinking about things I might tell him, not having fully absorbed the lesson that Gabe had already taught me on how inadequate my own imagination was.

"Your father is in Houston," he said.

"That's right," I said slowly, beginning to realize that this was going in a different direction than I had anticipated.

"When I'm in Houston, your father can help me," he said. "So I want to help you now. Just tell me what you want, and I'll get it for you."

I was taken aback by his directness, and horrified by the idea of putting my father in debt to Gabe. I thought about the potential of the situation, and a part of me wanted to laugh. Gabe didn't understand American culture at all, much less my father. It didn't matter what he did for me; if he showed up on my father's doorstep expecting to be taken to a brothel, my father would fertilize the lawn with him.

"There's really nothing I want," I said.

Frustration contorted Gabe's face. "Listen," he said, "I'll do anything for you. I *want* to do something for you. Just tell me what you want. Anything." He paused, and then, perhaps thinking that I didn't understand what he was getting at, added with a twinkle in his eye, "Girls?" The glint in his eye communicated a deeper question—an accusation—that he didn't need to say out loud. Was I secretly interested in the sort of entertainment that the Hollywood Club offered? Did I want to go back again without Hudson's knowledge?

I just stared back at him, hiding my thoughts.

"Boys?" he asked, grinning broadly.

"No," I said.

"Tell me what you want!"

He was getting agitated now, and I was more desperate than ever for him to leave. But I just didn't have the guts to tell him to get out. I was his teacher, and age be damned, it would have been entirely culturally appropriate for me to yell at him and tell him to leave. But that just wasn't my way. Fortunately, Evan possessed the perspicacity that Gabe lacked. He had clearly been embarrassed to accompany Gabe on this errand in the first place, and he must have suspected that Gabe's mission would fail. At last, he opened his mouth, having apparently decided that enough was enough.

"I think we need to go," he said.

"No!" Gabe shouted.

They argued heatedly in Chinese for a few more moments, and I began to wonder whether my living room was about to get torn apart in a fight. But this time, thankfully, Evan won, and he escorted a frowning Gabe out of my room, apologizing to me on the way out. When they were gone, I closed the door and breathed a sigh of relief, hoping that this would be Gabe's final attempt to put me in his debt, and marveling at how different these students were from the previous semester's lot.

15

Girls

My Sunday routine hadn't changed. Just as in the fall, I
went to church in the morning, Bible study at Gary's
in the afternoon, and English lessons with the translation
team in the evening. One Sunday morning in late February,
as often happened, yet another girl sat beside me while I was
waiting for the church service to begin. She looked at me and
smiled warmly.

"Hello," she said in Chinese.

When I replied, she asked me for my name. I gave it to
her and asked hers in return. It was Lifei. She reminded me
for a moment of Xingmei, the girl with the hazel eyes I'd met
in church the previous semester. But as I looked more closely,
I realized Lifei was different from Xingmei in every way.

Whereas Xingmei was dark and slim, Lifei was pale and had pudgy cheeks, with a Marilyn-Monroe-style mole on one of them. Xingmei had been a loud, fast talker, but Lifei spoke slowly and softly. When talking to her, I felt as if I had more opportunities to contribute to the conversation. And whereas Xingmei had been subtle and conservative, Lifei was . . . brazen.

From the very beginning, it was clear that Lifei was more interested in me than in the sermon, as she kept looking at me and smiling. Her perfume was strong, and her makeup was thick. And when her leg—smooth, and bare below a very short skirt—brushed mine, I was certain that it was intentional. For the second time, I wondered whether Chinese mothers taught their daughters how to seduce men.

Lifei's approach wasn't as effective as Xingmei's. With Xingmei—when she wasn't talking, anyway—I had felt as if I were under a gentle spell. But with Lifei, I felt as though cupid had exchanged his bow for a piano; only, rather than playing music on it, he had picked it up and was beating me over the head with it. From the start, I just wanted to get away.

Still, I was concerned for her spiritual wellbeing—or so I told myself—and at the end of the service I bought her a Bible and introduced her to the Christian girls I knew at the church. I wasn't planning to exchange phone numbers, but she asked for mine before she left, and as usual, I couldn't bring myself to refuse.

She called me in the middle of the following week, and I found that even over the phone, she was much easier to talk to than Xingmei. She chose simple words, and she spoke them slowly enough that I could understand. I was able to answer her questions with more than just the awkward "uh's" that I had offered Xingmei. At the end of the conversation, Lifei said she would talk to me later.

Indeed, she did call me again later. I had added her number to my contact list, so I knew it was her when I answered. Still, I felt awkward and uncertain, so I said "uh" before saying "hello" in Chinese. Immediately, she took offense.

"You don't know who I am?" she asked.

"Yes, I do!" I said.

"Then why did you say, 'Who are you?'"

"I didn't!"

"Yes you did!"

"No, I said 'Uh, hello.'"

"Exactly!"

We were both silent for a minute, and I thought about what I'd just said. I realized that putting "uh" and the Chinese for "hello" together gives you something that does sound an awful lot like, "Who is this?" So it seemed that I had just admitted to asking who she was—and there was really no recovering from that. Before I could think of anything else to say, though, she spoke again.

"Are you going to church again on Sunday?" she asked.

"Yes," I said.

"I'll see you there," she said, and hung up.

The next Sunday, I arrived at church early again. Lifei was nowhere that I could see, and I went ahead and took a seat. A few minutes later, *another* girl sat next to me. Apart from a couple of teeth that appeared to be trying to escape from her mouth, I thought she was fairly cute. She, too, smiled and said hello, and we chatted while waiting for the service to begin. Her name was Liujun.

Just when I was beginning to think that Lifei wasn't going to make it, she walked in the door. Her eyes swept around the room, and she smiled when she saw me. She walked over and then looked from me to the seats on either side of me. The one on my right was occupied by an old man; and Liujun was in the seat on my left. Lifei's smile faded.

"Hi, Lifei," I said. "This is Liujun."

They greeted each other, but Lifei did not look pleased. It was probably bad enough that I hadn't waited outside for her; and it was certainly worse that I was with another girl. But it must have been unforgivable that I let Lifei sit on the other side of this new girl from me. Liujun seemed oblivious to Lifei's mood, and she continued talking to me until the service started.

We sang the hymns, recited the Apostle's Creed and the Lord's Prayer, and then listened to the sermon in silence. When the sermon was over, announcements were made, followed by a benediction, and the congregation was dismissed. I now had to decide what to do about the two girls beside me.

"How about if we eat lunch together?" I suggested in Chinese.

"That sounds good," said Liujun.

Lifei, however, shook her head. "I have something else I

need to do," she said.

Without another word, she left, and I was standing alone with Liujun, who was smiling up at me. I hadn't intended to go out alone with a girl, but there was no backing out now. So I led the way down the stairs, out of the church, and across the street to the California Beef Noodle King.

We chatted as we walked, and I discovered that unlike Xingmei or Lifei, Liujun was actually interested in practicing English. She didn't know very many words, and her pronunciation was atrocious, but at least she wanted to try. I liked that. Over bowls of noodles, we chatted about our backgrounds. I asked her where she was from, and she told me that she was from Henan, a province that she said was famous for kung fu. Then I asked her what kind of work she did.

"I am looking for a job," she said.

"What kind of job?" I asked.

"I want to be a *zhuchi*," she said.

"What?" I asked.

"A hostess," she said in English. "Like on TV."

I looked at her for a moment, trying to understand what exactly she meant by that. The first thing I thought of was Billy Crystal hosting the Oscars. And then David Letterman. And then Bob Saget, from *America's Funniest Home Videos*. It sounded to me like a pretty ill-defined goal. After all, there was no tried-and-true path to becoming a TV hostess as far as I knew.

"Oh," I said at last. "Well, I'm looking for a job too, for next year." I had decided that I wanted to return to China independently. I liked ESI, but I wanted to follow the advice of the Apostle Paul and earn my own keep as a "tentmaker." I would keep serving the church and sharing the Gospel with those around me, but I could do so while working an ordinary job as an English teacher—or whatever else I could find.

When we finished eating, we walked along the promenade toward the bus stop on the main street. On the way there, Liujun held up a hand to indicate that she wanted to stop for a moment and that I was to wait for her. As I stood there and watched, she hocked up a loogie and sent it flying masterfully into a nearby trash can. She then looked up at me and flashed an adorable smile.

We went our separate ways, and I didn't hear from her again until the following Friday, when she called me. "Can you help me translate my résumé into English?" she asked.

"Sure," I said.

So on Saturday afternoon, she came over to Sinopec. I was walking her to my office, where we could load her résumé on my computer, when she appeared to remember something suddenly and began rummaging through her purse.

"I have something for you," she said.

She removed a folded-up piece of paper that looked as if it had been torn out of a magazine and held it out for me to see. It appeared to be a page of advertisements, and it was entirely in Chinese. One small advertisement had been circled in pen, and Liujun pointed to it, waiting for me to read it.

"What is it?" I asked.

"It's a job advertisement," she said in Chinese. "They are

looking for a foreigner."

"Oh! Thanks," I said. "What kind of job?"

"It doesn't say," she replied. Then, after a long pause, she said, "Actually, it's probably fake. A lot of these advertisements are scams."

"Oh," I said. "Well, thanks."

By the time we had translated her résumé and left my office, it was dark outside. On the way to the campus exit, she asked me a question that caught me off guard.

"Do you like George Bush?"

I hesitated. I had voted for Bush, as all good conservative Christians had done, thinking that his faith would make him a reliable leader. As I pondered how to answer Liujun's question, I remembered hearing a song on a Christian radio station that included a clip of some words Bush had spoken in a debate. When asked who his favorite philosopher was, he answered, "Christ—because he changed my life." Hearing those words in that song had brought tears to my eyes—and, I was now beginning to realize, probably a lot of other people's eyes, too, for entirely different reasons.

I had thought that Bush would make the world a better place; but now, the war in Iraq had been dragging on for two years, and the situation was promising to get uglier. I was well aware that Bush had an abysmal reputation abroad; and as I looked at Liujun, I could see in her eyes what her opinion of him was. It clearly wasn't favorable.

"I think he has good intentions," I said at last.

"Do you think he's a real Christian?" she asked.

"Yes."

"I don't," she said firmly. "A real Christian wouldn't do what he's doing in Iraq."

As I stood there looking down at Liujun, I desperately wanted to defend Bush's actions. I wanted to explain why America had invaded Iraq. I wanted to show her that there were good reasons for the war and that the consequences would ultimately be good. But my Chinese was far too poor to accomplish these things; and moreover, I wasn't sure I could convince *myself* that they were true. So I said nothing.

I walked Liujun the rest of the way to the light rail station, and as we waited for the train to come, I asked her where she lived. She said her apartment was only two stops away, in the direction I would be traveling when going to church. This seemed like a good opportunity.

"How about if we ride to church together on Sunday?" I asked.

"Okay," she said.

Thus on the following two Sundays, we rode to church together. It was a twenty-five-minute subway ride, followed by a twenty-minute bus ride, so it gave us plenty of time to talk. I found it to be quite fun the first time, but by the second Sunday, we had run out of things to talk about, and much of the ride passed in uncomfortable silence. Nevertheless, I was still preparing to ride with her for a third time, when she called me.

"I will come pick you up," she said.

"You have a car?" I asked.

"No. A friend will drive."

I waited at the front gate of the institute, wondering what Liujun's friend would be like. Perhaps she would be prettier than Liujun. I tried to suppress that thought and focus instead on the fact that this would be an opportunity to share the Gospel with yet another person. I took the whole situation as a good sign for Liujun's spiritual status, as she evidently liked church enough to invite a friend. Perhaps she would soon be saved.

I had been waiting for quite some time when an old, dented car with faded, peeling paint pulled up in front of me. Liujun rolled down the window and waved enthusiastically for me to hop in the back seat. It wasn't until I got in that Liujun introduced me to her friend.

His name was Li Chen, and he was a shady-looking guy with eyes that appeared to be always narrowed in suspicion. They kept shifting about erratically, giving me the impression that he was accustomed to being on the lookout for cops. His voice sounded like a desiccated carcass being dragged across rocky desert ground, and as we drove I could easily see why: He chain-smoked, always lighting up his next cigarette before the last one went out.

However emphatically I had been telling myself that I was not pursuing romance with Liujun, it was a bit of blow to be relegated quite literally to the back seat while she and Li Chen engaged in casual conversation that I couldn't even follow. They chatted and laughed, occasionally glancing back toward me as if to make sure I hadn't died.

At last, there came a break in their laughter, and I tried to reassert my presence. Despite my negative feelings toward Li Chen, I was resolved to do my Christian duty and either share the Gospel with him if he wasn't already a believer or be a brother to him if he was.

"Are you a Christian?" I asked him.

"No," he said.

I was ready with a follow-up: "Is this your first time going to church?"

"I'm not going to church," he said.

At this, I was surprised. I looked at Liujun.

"He's just giving us a ride," she said.

"Oh."

I felt like an idiot. Still, I wasn't ready to give up.

"What kind of work do you do?" I asked.

His cancerous vocal cords rasped something that was un-intelligible to me. I looked to Liujun for a rasp-to-Chinese translation, and she gave a long explanation that I wasn't able to understand fully. Li Chen worked for a company that made packaging or printed labels on boxes or something. Whatever it was, I decided that making interesting conversation about it would have been beyond me even in English, so I fell silent again, hoping to arrive at the church soon. We did, and Liujun and I stepped out of the car.

"What did you think of Li Chen?" Liujun asked as soon as he had driven away.

"He's not bad," I lied. But inside, I was thinking, "All jealousy aside, I hope for your sake that you don't end up with him."

"I think so, too," she said.

When church was over, Li Chen was there waiting, cigarette in mouth, shifty eyes surveying the promenade. Liujun waved goodbye to me, and they walked toward his car together. I had a feeling she had been choosing between Li Chen and me, and she had just now made her final decision. I could have been wrong—I might never have been in the equation at all—but as it turned out, I never saw Liujun again.

By this point, I couldn't help thinking that maybe I was turning girls away from Christ. This could have been viewed as a good thing; one of the "problems" in the Chinese church was the gender imbalance—by some counts, the church was three-quarters female—and by decreasing the number of female churchgoers, I was helping to solve it. But as a missionary, I was attacking the wrong side of the equation. I should have been concentrating on getting more *men* to come to church rather than reducing the number of women. With this in mind, I decided that it would be a good idea to stop talking to girls at church.

16

Boundaries

This wasn't the first time I'd lain in bed, weak and trembling from an extended bout with food poisoning, waiting for a girl to come visit me. Over the winter holiday, Bibo—the girl Hudson and I had met on the train to Tai'An so long ago—had happened to call me just as I was catching my breath between fits of vomiting. Upon learning that I was sick, she had rushed over to boil water for me and force me to swallow a handful of pills that looked suspiciously like rabbit droppings before departing with a stern admonition never to tell her boyfriend that she had been there.

But this time was different. The girl I was expecting didn't have a vindictive boyfriend (as far as I knew), and this time *I* had been the one to initiate contact, by sending a message saying I was ill. Despite the experience with Bibo, I hadn't anticipated that this girl too would want to visit me—she lived about an hour and a half away—but she insisted on coming. Girls visiting guys afflicted by food poisoning was evidently a thing in China, and she would not be deterred.

I had met her in church on Easter Sunday, despite my recent resolution to stop talking to girls there. It hadn't been my fault, really; even though we had been standing next to each other in line, and even though she looked familiar, I didn't say a word to her. It was Gary—the guy whose Bible study I had been attending—who came over and spoiled my virtuous silence. On his way to the end of the line, he stopped and introduced us to each other—or reintroduced us, rather, since it turned out that this was the same pretty, pensive girl named Leila who had been at the first Bible study I'd attended. I couldn't very well avoid talking to her after the introduction, and we ended up sitting together during the service.

That might have been the end of it; but when it was time to go, Leila asked me if I could show her the way to the bus stop—which was a bit odd, since I was the foreigner, and besides, she had been to the church many times before. I showed her the way, and once there, it seemed only natural to give her my phone number and ask her to send me a message when she got home so I would know she had arrived safely.

The words "good night," when received from a girl just before bed time, turned out to be beautifully intoxicating. And "good morning" was even better. After only one or two weeks, I had accumulated quite a few text messages from her, which it pleased me to read when I was feeling bored or lonely. And that was why I thought to text her when I got sick.

My illness, severe though it was, didn't prevent me from making the hike across campus and over a footbridge to meet Leila at the light rail station. The first thing I noticed when she came out through the turnstile was that she was wearing a dress. It struck me as odd, because even at church she had seemed like a jeans-and-T-shirt kind of girl.

As soon as she saw me, her face lit up.

We walked back to campus, and then, together with Hudson—I had invited him along as a chaperone in order to avoid violating ESI's no-dating policy—we went to a nearby restaurant to have dinner. We were halfway through our meal before I noticed that some of my students were there as well. Despite being in their mid-thirties, they pointed and giggled like kindergartners at the sight of their teacher eating with a girl. One of them, Lance, walked over to us, his face split in two by a giant grin, and talked for a while before heading back to report his findings to his classmates.

After the meal, Hudson felt reasonably certain that Leila and I weren't going to do anything ungodly, and he went to his room, leaving me to walk Leila back to the light rail station on my own. As we walked, I made a conscious effort to stay between her and the rush of traffic on the street. It was a gentleman's rule I had been taught long ago. She noticed, and said it was thoughtful of me. I looked again at her dress and wondered . . . had she put it on just for me?

The next morning, Lance stood before my class and

announced that he had spotted me the previous evening with a girl—a Chinese girl. He was grinning with smug satisfaction, clearly quite proud to be the bearer of this valuable piece of gossip. "She had a face," he said, pausing for dramatic effect, "like an apple."

"Oooh," said several of the students.

The following weeks were busy. I was interviewing for teaching jobs for the next school year, and my parents came for a ten-day visit. I took them to all the attractions around Beijing—Tiananmen Square, the Forbidden City, the Great Wall, and the Summer Palace—and then to Xi'An, the ancient capital where Emperor Qin had been buried more than 2,200 years before in an underground necropolis with over 8,000 life-sized terra cotta warriors to guard him in the afterlife.

On the last day of my parents' visit, I brought them to my English class and opened up the floor for questions. There seemed to be only one topic the students cared about.

"How would you feel if your son married a Chinese girl?" asked one.

"Will you buy a house for your son if he marries a Chinese girl?" asked another. It was, after all, the Chinese custom for the groom's parents to buy a house for the new couple. My mom was shocked. I wondered whether my students would have asked those questions if Lance hadn't just seen me in that restaurant with Leila. Were they thinking of her? I certainly was.

When my birthday arrived, Leila bought me a gift. I had been told that Chinese people didn't give gifts for birthdays, so I was somewhat surprised. It was a plaque engraved with a quote of Hudson Taylor, the most famous missionary ever to go to China. "I used to ask God to help me," it said. "Then I asked if I might help him. I ended up by asking God to do his work through me."

Before long, those little messages that Leila and I sent each morning and evening eclipsed all my other sources of happiness. I was more excited about her than I had ever felt about Nellie. But overshadowing all of my excitement was a deep, troubling sense that what I was doing was wrong—that I was violating my contract with ESI. I could tell myself all I wanted that we weren't dating. But what mattered, in my mind, was that I was knowingly trying to build a romance through those messages.

It had to stop.

I called Lillian, my supervisor at ESI, to confess the whole situation. She thanked me for sharing so openly with her; and then she told me to set whatever limits I thought appropriate. After we hung up, I stared down at my phone. The next call was going to be much harder.

My heart raced. I had called Leila many times on the phone, but never before to tell her that I "liked" her—which I obviously had to do if I was going to tell her that we could not date. Somehow, that made everything different. This was going to be what we evangelicals called the "defining-the-relationship talk," or DTR for short.

I dialed her number and waited while I listened to the strangely pure ringtone that only America doesn't use. She answered as she always did, with a melodic "hello" that told me there was no one she'd rather receive a call from than me. Hands shaking, I came right out and told her how I felt. And then I waited.

Silence.

What I wanted—needed—was confirmation that she felt the same about me. It should have been obvious—after all, had she not asked me to take her to the bus stop on Easter, and had she not reciprocated every step of the way? But I was nervous nonetheless. What if, in her eyes, all of our interactions had been nothing more than normal acts of platonic friendship? Or what if she felt the same way but decided in the end that she just couldn't get involved with a foreigner? When I finished talking, I could hardly breathe as I waited for her response.

"I like you, too," she said.

Relief and joy flooded over me.

And then I slammed her with the terms of my contract and the limitations that I felt it necessary to impose on our relationship. Until my contract expired—that would be in only three weeks, but it seemed like an eternity at the moment—we wouldn't be able to date. Moreover, I said, our recent interactions had already been pushing the boundaries. I proceeded to describe in precise detail the restrictions that I thought we needed to place on our activities.

There could be no more "good morning" or "good night" text messages. In fact, text messages would only be allowed if we needed to talk about something important, which we could then do over the phone. But we could only have one phone conversation per week. Oh, and only one email per week, as well. And most important of all, we were to have no in-person interaction except at church and Bible study.

"I agree with these things completely," she said.

Almost before we had hung up, I logged onto Amazon and ordered a book called *The Ten Commandments of Dating* and another called *Intercultural Marriage*. I signed up for a weekly email publication that provided creative ideas for romantic gifts and activities. I was determined to get things right when my contract with ESI expired and we began officially dating.

During the remaining three weeks of the semester, it was difficult for me to focus on my teaching—or anything else for that matter. My only concern was to finish without disaster. And there should have been no reason I couldn't do so. Despite the class monitor's objections to *The Rookie* and Gabe's misguided attempts to ingratiate himself with me, everything was going smoothly.

But then one of my students began causing problems.

The student, a cherubic guy in his mid-twenties who had chosen the name Jason, had never been particularly diligent to begin with. And now, suddenly, he stopped doing his work entirely, and his participation in class activities became reluctant at best. I pulled him aside to address the problem.

"If you don't turn in your assignments," I said, "you're going to fail the course."

"I don't care," he said with a shrug.

I blinked. I wouldn't have thought there was a student in China who could fail a course without caring. And furthermore, I had been told that the English class I was teaching was a mandatory component of Sinopec's MBA program. Surely Jason cared at least a little about *that*. "Don't you need to pass this course in order to finish your MBA?" I asked.

"No," he said.

He was as nonchalant as could be. He wasn't bluffing about not caring, and that meant it would be difficult to find an argument that might sway him. As I thought about how to respond, a memory floated up from a few weeks earlier. One of the class monitors, Andre, had said something odd to me in an offhand way: "Jason has no respect." At the time, I hadn't bothered to ask him what exactly he meant by that, but I now thought that perhaps I could appeal to the value of respect to get Jason to do his work. After all, in China, people were said to respect and revere teachers. It was a Confucian virtue.

"Well, your attitude is disrespectful," I said, "both to me and your classmates."

"Excuse me?" he said.

In a flash, his nonchalance had evaporated. Thinking that my tactic was working, I repeated myself. Then I watched as he took a deep breath and formulated his response. A fire now burned in his eyes.

"It is true that I have no respect for you," he said slowly. "But how have I been disrespectful to my classmates?"

This was even more shocking than his apathy. No one in

China *ever* said directly to a teacher, "I have no respect for you." Clearly, Jason saw no reason why he should even pretend to have respect for me, and he wasn't going to argue the point at all. But he seemed *highly* concerned about being accused of disrespecting his *classmates*. I had no idea where to go from there, so I punted.

"I suggest you go talk to Andre about it," I said.

That afternoon, I received a phone call from Andre. He said that Jason wanted to meet with both of us in the library to discuss my accusation. With much dread, I walked to the library and found the two of them sitting at a table, waiting. When Jason saw me, his fury was plain on his face. He launched into what sounded like a prepared speech, demanding that I apologize for accusing him of disrespecting his classmates.

I looked at Andre in disbelief and saw that he didn't want to be there any more than I did. He was just hoping to smooth things over, and he didn't seem to know how to deal with Jason either. Meanwhile, in the face of Jason's attitude, I was feeling less and less inclined to budge. It was ludicrous that he could say to my face, "I have no respect for you," and then demand an apology.

So I refused.

The conversation went nowhere, and very soon it was over entirely. "I will make sure you pay for this," Jason said at last. And with that, he got up and walked out of the library.

I sat in silence with Andre for a while, and then he looked up at me and asked, "Do you know the book *The Ugly*

American?"

"Yes," I said.

I had heard my students talking about it before and looked it up. It was a book about how obnoxious Americans are when they live and travel abroad, making terrible impressions on people all over the world—especially in Asia. I had been hoping that it wasn't *my* behavior that sparked their discussion of the book.

"Well," Andre said, "there's also a book called *The Ugly Chinaman*." I just looked at him blankly for a moment, wondering what he was getting at. Finally, Andre pointed in the direction in which Jason had gone. "He is the ugly Chinaman," he said.

After that, I was waiting for something bad to happen, despite Andre's reassurances. I suspected that Jason's father—or some family member—had a high position in the company. That was probably how he had secured his job at Sinopec in the first place. How else could he have risen to a managerial position at such a young age, with his attitude and work ethic? Perhaps he really could make me "pay" somehow.

For the remaining weeks, Jason continued attending class as usual. His attitude did not change, but he made no more demands and caused no trouble that I could see. I gave him exactly the grade that he earned, though I was certain it really would have no impact on him. Perhaps the English class wasn't really an essential component of the MBA program, or an administrator would be bribed to change his transcript. In any case, it was out of my hands.

When the semester came to a close, our students organized the sort of banquet that I was now accustomed to. The main attraction of the evening was, of course, the *baijiu*, but I drank only beer. Near the end, when a large fraction of the students were stumbling around and slurring their speech, Jason approached me, carrying his glass of *baijiu*. Red-faced, he held it up in front of me.

"Mr. Rambow," he said, "please drink with me."

"Don't drink with him!" cried several other students.

I looked around the room. Andre was shaking his head. Then I looked back at Jason.

"Please," he said.

I hesitated. I was hoping never to see Jason again, but who knew what the future held? If his last memory of me was my refusal to drink with him, perhaps he would be even more determined to "make me pay" somehow. On the other hand, if he remembered my willingness to drink with him despite his blatant disrespect, perhaps things would go well if our paths ever crossed again.

That might have been enough reason to drink with him, but there was another argument that was much more important to me: I wanted to be able to love my enemy as Christ had commanded. If I refused to drink, I would be showing that I, too, allowed myself to be controlled by petty grudges. I was better than that, and I wanted to show it.

So I drank.

I don't know what all of the other students thought. Who knew what Jason had said about me, or what strings he had pulled to try to cause me trouble? The other students surely had good reason to shout for me not to drink with him. And perhaps drinking with him made me look like a fool in their eyes. But in my mind, that was when I won.

Much more important than my victory over Jason, however, was the fact that my contract with ESI had expired at last. I was free to begin dating. I could go out with Leila now. Time was critical, though. Between her work schedule and my upcoming flight back to America, we would only have two days together before I left Beijing. I had to make each of them count.

On the first day, I took her to Beihai Park—the default first-date destination for uncreative men. There we rented a boat and rowed out into the middle of the lake, where we talked about our vision for our future and shared our reservations about having an intercultural relationship. I was afraid people would think I was one of those guys with "yellow fever" who had come to China just for the girls. And Leila said she had been worrying people would assume she was just getting involved with a foreigner for money or an American visa. "But I finally decided that I just don't care what other people think," she said.

At the end of the evening, I walked her once more to a bus stop. We hadn't kissed, or even held hands—such behavior wouldn't have been appropriate on a first date—but as she boarded the bus for her apartment, I looked at the back of her shoulders, at the way her red-tinged hair flowed over them.

This is my future wife, I thought.

The next day would be our last together before I left. I had gotten her a parting gift, a brown beaded bracelet that had a sort of Chinese poem on it:

Flowers blossom,
Honor and prosperity,
Friendship forever.

It was pretty, but the more I thought about it, the more inadequate it seemed. I had to give her something more, something personal—something that would remind her of me every day. But it was late already, and the stores were closed; so whatever I decided on, I would have to make it myself.

I surveyed my resources. I had little more than a blank sketch pad and some colored pens. Then an idea hit me. I counted the number of days that we would be apart over the summer and found that there would be exactly fifty. I counted the pages in the sketch pad: fifty-two. That was it: I would make a calendar with one page for each day.

I uncapped a pen and began writing with my best calligraphy. Leila and I had been memorizing verses from the book of Proverbs together, so I put a proverb on each page, along with a note of encouragement. On the cover, I drew a cat—she liked cats and had introduced me to the phenomenon of cat videos on the internet. Fifty pages of calligraphy took longer than I anticipated, and I ended up working on the calendar all night.

The next day, Leila and I attended church and Gary's

Bible study before going out together once more. In the evening, I escorted her home, and just outside her apartment, I gave her the calendar and the bracelet. For a long moment, she stood there staring at the calendar—or rather, through it. "Don't open it yet," I told her. "You can only look at one page each day. Okay?"

"Okay," she said.

With that, it was time for me to go, and I hailed a taxi. After we hugged and I got in, Leila closed the door gently and then touched the window with her fingertips to say goodbye. The beads on her new bracelet clicked against the glass, and the car began moving. I watched her shrink into the distance, knowing that I wouldn't see her again for fifty days.

17

Fifty Days Apart

The congregation at my home church in Houston was bubbling with excitement on the day that I returned. But the furor had nothing to do with me; there was another missionary who had just returned from Russia, and he was going to speak in place of the pastor about the miraculous work God had been doing there.

The stories the man told were incredible. He had been organizing Billy-Graham-style crusades all over the country, and at each one, vast numbers of attendees had "indicated decisions" to accept Christ as their savior. Three thousand souls saved here; five thousand there; and even ten thousand at one event. It was clear that—largely due to this man's service—a great revival was afoot, and Russia would soon be transformed into a bastion of Christianity.

The message sounded familiar. People had been saying the same about China for some time. The 2003 bestseller *Jesus in Beijing* had predicted that within three decades, fully one third of China's population would be Christian, and even the highest leaders in the land would be seeking God's guidance for their people. It was the sort of thing evangelicals ate up with relish. But a small voice inside me whispered that perhaps these messengers were only telling us what we wanted to hear.

As I listened to the presentation, the skeptic within me rose up. The guy was a showman. How different were his crusades in Russia from the performance he was giving right now? Of what, exactly, did those "decisions" to accept Christ consist? A raised hand in response to the question, "Who will give himself to Christ?" A checked box on a response card? How substantial was this man's work, really?

Part of my skepticism was due to envy—the man clearly had a more successful ministry than I did—but not all of it. I had once believed the only thing that counted was a "decision" to accept Christ. That was, after all, what "saved" a person and put them on the path to heaven rather than hell. But I knew that such decisions could be fleeting things. Ministries that focused on getting people to pray the "sinner's prayer" now seemed shallow to me.

After the service, I felt unable to connect with my friends. They were raving about the report we had just heard. How great God's work in Russia was! How blessed we were to have a hand in it, since our church was supporting it with both prayer and money! Praise God that our missionaries were returning with such news!

I didn't imagine for a second that anyone might be comparing me unfavorably to that missionary from Russia. But—despite my skepticism of his work—I couldn't keep from doing so myself. I, too, had received money and prayer support from this congregation. But my service had yielded no fruit that I could see. I had not led a single soul to Christ.

I knew that I shouldn't be so hard on myself. I had been in the field less than a year, whereas the speaker from Russia had been serving for over a decade. And although I hadn't converted anyone, I still had plenty to report about all the wonderful things God was doing in the Three-Self Church. And I was eager to take my ministry to a higher level.

The next day, I called the church office and asked to arrange a meeting with the pastor. I wanted to talk to him about building connections with the church in China and creating new ministry opportunities. The receptionist assured me that the pastor would be excited about my ideas and told me to email him. After I hung up, I spent an hour composing an email and sent it. All I had to do now was wait.

In the meantime, I had a girl to woo. I emailed Leila pictures of flowers that I had picked, sent her recordings of me playing the piano, and called her as often as I could. I told her about my Chinese studies and my plans for ministry. She emailed me selfies from church events, shared cat videos with me, and told me about life at the architecture firm where she worked.

She also told me about a guy who kept asking her out, and for the first time ever, I was jealous. Even when Mark had started dating Nellie again after giving me his blessing to pursue her, I hadn't felt this way. Somewhat nervously, I told her how I felt. The next day, she emailed me—and *thanked* me for my jealousy. She also said that she had taken care of the problem permanently. "I told him that I never wanted to talk to him again," she said.

I interpreted the smooth development of our relationship as evidence that it was God's will for us to be together. Sometimes you knew which path God wanted you to take because he would open doors along that path, making your way smooth and easy. And other times, the appearance of obstacles proved you were going in the right direction because either God was testing you or Satan was trying to stop you. No one ever said aloud that this reasoning could be used to justify any action at all.

My confidence didn't falter until I was at a party thrown by an old middle school friend. There were dozens of people I'd never met before, and a lot of them were girls. I chatted with several, and as I did so, I began to get a horrible, sinking feeling. English flowed freely and easily from their lips. They laughed with me over American cultural references. When I said, "You know what I mean?" I felt like they *really* knew what I meant based on our shared experience of growing up and going to school in America.

I put my hand in my pocket and tightly clutched my

wallet, in which I kept a photograph of Leila. I knew that my Chinese would never reach a native level, and neither would her English. Could she and I ever connect as closely as I could with an American girl—or as closely as she could with a Chinese guy? The possibility that I had made a mistake in making my interest known to her loomed over me like the threat of damnation itself, and it made me want to vomit. I left the party early in the morning haunted by the thought.

I started having nightmares after that. They contained no threat of violence, no embarrassment, no invisible pursuers. Instead, they were dreams of ordinary life in America. I had an American wife, or girlfriend, and a good job. Everything was normal. But Leila wasn't there. There was just a distant, nagging memory of a girl in China that I had left behind without ever looking back—a girl I had abandoned, whose name I didn't even remember.

No dream had ever made me feel worse.

At the same time, I was making my way through the book I'd bought on intercultural marriage. It described so many challenges that one was likely to face in such a relationship. The author had, of course, been in one herself—but she had gotten a divorce. What could that mean except that she had decided in the end that it wasn't worth it?

With these worries gnawing at me, I flew to California to help train the new ESI teachers. When I arrived, they were in the middle of the "low expectations" campaign. I saw some of my friends sit in front of the next crop of teachers and tell a new set of horror stories. Several of the trainees asked me whether it was really that bad. And for many of my colleagues, I realized, it *had* been that bad—but there had been good experiences, too.

I connected especially well with two of the new teachers in particular. One was a guy named Matthew who was about my age, and the other was a retired guy named Warren. As it turned out, they would be taking Hudson's and my places at Sinopec in the fall, so it was likely I would see a lot more of them during the coming year when I returned to Beijing.

Matthew was into the Prosperity Gospel. He showed me a picture of a particular model of private jet and said, "That's the kind of plane I'm going to have in the future." He was "believing for it," and he spoke with confidence that God would give it to him because of his faith. Another time, when I asked him about his political views, he said, "Well, I know I'm going to have a lot of money eventually, so I might as well vote for the party that's going to lower my taxes."

Both Matthew and Warren were Pentecostals, which meant they believed in baptism by the Holy Spirit and speaking in tongues. I recalled my conversation with Andrés—the guy who had first told me about speaking in tongues at that Campus Crusade for Christ retreat so long ago—and my desire to be filled with the Holy Spirit one day. So I asked them about it.

They were both adamant that baptism by the Spirit was something that any Christian could receive. There was nothing magical or exclusive about it; you simply needed someone who was already filled with the Spirit to place his hands on you and pray for you. It wasn't a necessary part of being a Christian, but it was certainly desirable. Warren himself had chosen to seek baptism by the Holy Spirit because he wanted "to take his relationship with God to the next level."

"The first time I spoke in tongues," Warren said, "I said the word 'lama'." He placed the stress on the second syllable, drawing it out. "It just came to me, and I repeated it over and over again. It turned out that it was one of the words Jesus had spoken on the cross when asking God, 'Why have you forsaken me?'"

This seemed to lend credibility to the claim that Warren was *really* speaking in tongues—and one with Biblical significance, at that. I wondered whether I, too, could speak ancient Aramaic or Hebrew, or some angelic language that had never been spoken by a human. I didn't get a chance to bring it up again at training, but I planned to ask about it again in Beijing.

In my next conversation with Leila, she told me that she had gone to my new apartment at the Semiconductor Institute, where I would be working that fall, and given it a thorough cleaning so that it would be in good condition when I returned. It was the most thoughtful thing anyone had ever done for me. That made me feel even worse about my wavering resolve; but it also made me think she was so wonderful that no cultural barrier could possibly matter.

On the final Sunday before my return to Beijing, the pastor at my church told a story to illustrate the depth of God's love for us. It was so moving that I felt compelled to share it with Leila, and as soon as I got home, I wrote her an email:

My pastor told us a story this morning. After an earthquake, a man learned that his son's school had been destroyed. He rushed to the school and found that it had been reduced to a pile of rubble. As other parents arrived, they immediately lost hope that their children might still be alive.

But the man ran to the area where his son's classroom had been, and he began to dig in the rubble. With his bare hands, he removed pieces of brick, stone, and metal. The police told him to stop digging. No one could have survived, they said.

He kept digging, though. His hands became bloody, and he didn't stop to eat or drink. When he had been digging for thirty-eight hours, he heard a voice under the rubble say, "Daddy, is that you?" It was his son.

The man said, "Yes, son, I'm here."

His son replied, "I knew you would come."

When I heard this story, I thought, "I will love Leila just as that man loved his son." If you are ever in trouble, I will do everything I can to come to you. And I want you to know, just as that man's son did, that I will come.

I hoped that Leila would be moved by my sentiment; but I could never have expected what she told me in her reply:

I've heard that story before. And when the son was under the rubble with the other children, he told them, "My dad will come to find me. He said if I'm in trouble he will come wherever I am."

Henry, I will trust you like that son trusted his father. I'm so thankful to the Lord that you have shared this with me. I read this story several years ago, and I hoped that one day someone would tell me I could trust him like this. I had almost forgotten about it, but never stopped waiting and hoping.

If that wasn't confirmation from God that Leila and I were meant to be together, then I didn't know what was. After that, my worries about language and cultural barriers vanished completely. I was certain that Leila would be the perfect partner for me in both life and ministry.

A few days later, I boarded a plane bound for China for the third time. On both previous occasions, I had been formally affiliated with a Christian organization. This time, it was still my intent to share the Gospel and serve the church. But now I was going to be completely independent.

I had become a rogue missionary.

18

Love and Hate

"Are you sure you want to do this?" I asked.

Leila returned my gaze over the remnants of our dinner, and I found myself thinking that this was the most pivotal question I had ever voiced. If she said yes, we would begin officially dating—which, to my mind, meant embarking on the journey toward marriage. If she said no, then everything between us would be over.

There was no middle ground.

My plane had landed just a few hours earlier, and after meeting at the airport—where we had both secretly feared that we would be unable to recognize each other—we had taken a taxi to my new apartment at the Institute of Semiconductors. Once there, I had proceeded to unload a pile of gifts for her from my suitcase, including a giant coffee mug, a stuffed Nemo, maps of America and Houston, and an English Bible that had dozens of love notes hidden between its pages. We had then taken a walk through the campus of the nearby Forestry University before coming to the restaurant in which we now sat.

The conversation had been serious from the start. After rehashing all of our previous discussions about the difficulties of an intercultural relationship, I had disclosed at last the vow that I had made to God so long ago—that I would become a minister—so that Leila would know what she was getting into. Now, with the big question having left my lips, the moment of truth had arrived.

"Yes," she said.

And so our fate was set.

I didn't tell her the reason for my vow—that it had been the plea of a terrified little boy bargaining for a few more years of life—and she didn't ask. I imagined that she assumed it to be a product of my piety and my confidence in God. In any case, her vision of what it might entail was not much different from my own. "I know that some day you might go to a faraway country to serve God," she said. "And I'll go with you."

Of course, I was already in that faraway country. After my experiences with Cru and ESI, I had an idea of what I might do to minister to China. Following the Apostle Paul's tent-making model, I would work a simple job—teaching English would do—while serving to facilitate missions from America to China. Beginning with friends from my college ministry and my home church, I would coordinate vision trips similar to the one that had first brought me over.

It wouldn't be hard to do. But developing such a ministry would take time. For now, in addition to building my new relationship with Leila, I needed to focus on getting settled in my new circumstances. That included developing the curriculum for the courses in scientific English that I would be teaching, learning the art of editing scientific manuscripts, and getting involved in my new community.

My neighborhood—the Semiconductor Institute—was surrounded by a dilapidated brick-and-concrete wall. Nearly everyone who worked at the institute also lived on campus, and it was a while before I realized that it was an actual commune, a remnant of a bygone era. That was when the connection between the words "commune" and "communism" finally sank in.

I quickly became known as "the foreigner"—because I was quite literally the only one there. My presence was the source of much excitement, and everyone, students and faculty alike, was eager to meet me. Despite being an introvert, I enjoyed my newfound popularity and made an effort to come out of my shell and immerse myself in the language and culture.

My Chinese had improved quite a bit since that debacle of a search for an internet café the previous year. On one occasion, I sat down beside a student in the cafeteria and asked where he'd gotten his bowl of porridge. At the sound of near-flawless Chinese on my tongue, his mouth fell open, and after taking in my blue eyes and enormous Western nose, he asked in disbelief, "Are you Chinese?"

But there were other occasions on which things didn't go quite so well. I spent a full two minutes in conversation with a taxi driver, thinking all the while that we were discussing the likelihood of being struck by lightning in a rainstorm, only to discover in the end that he had been directing me to a convenience store where I could get change. And once, when trying to order a drink, I accidentally asked a waitress to bring me a large-breasted girl.

When classes began, I started out just as I had done at Sinopec, asking the students to choose an English name and prepare a short speech to introduce themselves to the class. The previous year, I had provided a list of common names for my students to choose from, but this time I decided to give them more freedom. I figured they were familiar with English names already and could easily find lists on the internet.

That turned out to be a mistake.

I learned that the Chinese approach to choosing a name was vastly different from the American approach. When Chinese parents or grandparents are looking for a name for a baby, the search often consists of flipping through a dictionary and picking characters with an interesting meaning or beautiful sound. Strange things tend to happen when this method is applied in English.

"My English name," declared one of my students at the beginning of his speech, "is Shakesapple. I like Shakespeare, and I like apples, so I put them together." Another student began his speech with, "You can call me Flying Ghost."

No, I can't, I thought.

My new students showed me the same hospitality that I had always experienced in China, and they seemed so full of joy that it was hard to believe they lacked something spiritually. If anything, I felt that *they* were ministering to *me*. They seemed so content, so fulfilled; and so I was a bit surprised when one student, named Byron, came to my office and hit me with a heavy question.

"What do you think about regrets in life?" he asked.

I stared back at him for a while in stunned silence. Who would ask such a question unless they felt burdened by some particular regret? It occurred to me that perhaps Byron had come to confide something in me, and perhaps this would be one of my first opportunities to be a minister. The best way to proceed, I thought, would be to open up a little myself.

"Well, I think everybody has regrets. I certainly do."

"What regrets do you have?" Byron asked.

I decided to tell him about a girlfriend I'd had in high school. As a born-again Christian, I now looked back on my relationship with her as "impure," and I regretted not just that, but the way I had treated her. When I finished speaking, Byron stared back at me for a while, and I imagined that he was preparing himself to confess some deep regret that had been weighing down on him.

"I think we should live life with no regrets," he said at last. "I have a friend who lives his life with no regrets," he continued. "He does something that a lot of other people would think is wrong. He . . . goes out . . . with businessmen. They come here and pick him up sometimes, and then they drop him off the next day."

Byron waited for his words to sink in before going on.

"These men buy nice things for my friend. He has some very fancy, expensive clothes. Other people wonder where he gets them, and I'm the only one who knows. But I look at my friend and see that he has no regrets, and I admire him. What do you think?"

He was smiling now, a strange smile, probing my face with his eyes. The cogs in my mind turned slowly. I was trying to understand why Byron would share this with me. Why would he care what I thought of his friend's activities? Unless . . .

I had noticed that Byron himself wore expensive clothes. Designer glasses. Could they have been acquired in the sort of business that he had just described to me? Was it really a *friend* that he had been talking about? Slowly, it dawned on me that the only reason for him to ask what I thought about such activities was to determine whether *I* was interested.

"I think," I said haltingly, "that's a bad idea."

After an uncomfortable silence, Byron nodded, stood, and then left without saying anything else. Perhaps I had misunderstood his intent, but for the rest of the semester, I couldn't look at him without thinking, *Wow. One of my students is a prostitute.*

Byron wasn't the only student who opened up to me in a surprising way. Within the first week of class, the two monitors—guys who had chosen the names Kevin and William—took me out to a restaurant that specialized in Peking Duck. Halfway through the meal, William suddenly diverted the conversation from the usual diplomatic banter to something much more inflammatory.

"What do you think about Japanese people?"

I was vaguely aware of a fair amount of ill will between China and Japan in relation to Japan's invasion of China during World War II. There had recently been news reports about the Japanese Prime Minister's visit to the Yasukuni Shrine, a war memorial that honored some of the Japanese military commanders who had been responsible for the "Rape of Nanjing." I was afraid of how touchy a subject it might prove to be, so I just said, "I don't know much about them," hoping that would put an end to it.

But William wasn't about to move on.

"I hate them," he said. "Do you know what they did to us?" I could hear strain in his voice. His face was beginning to turn red, and I didn't think it was from the alcohol.

"I've heard a little," I replied.

William shook his head. He wanted me to know the full extent of the crimes committed by Japan, and he proceeded to describe them in graphic detail. Kevin listened in silence while William went on at some length about torture, mass beheadings, and rape. At the end of it all, William looked me in the eye and hardened his voice even further, if that was possible. "I hope that one day in the future we will go to war with Japan. I hope for the opportunity to join the army and go kill as many Japanese as I can."

The conversation was subdued for the remainder of the meal. When we were done, I watched as William and Kevin fought over who would pay the bill, and after William won, we walked back to the institute. I thanked them for the lunch, and William went inside his building. But Kevin lingered for a moment. "I want you to know," he said, "that most Chinese people do not think that way."

In later weeks, however, I did run into other students who had similar feelings—and had no qualms expressing them to a foreigner. One student told me that Japanese children were taught in school that they must destroy China when they grow up. Another told me about a friend of his who had vowed that if China ever went to war with Japan, he would donate half of his salary to finance it; and if there was ever a war with Taiwan, he would give his whole salary.

The intensity of their hatred for Japan stunned me. The Nanjing massacre had happened sixty-eight years earlier. Both the victims and the perpetrators were nearly all dead. In my mind, Japan's crimes were similar to those the Nazis had committed against the Jews, and I had never heard any of my Jewish friends talk this way about Germans.

I sensed that something was different about the situation between China and Japan, but I couldn't see what it was. All I knew was that the wounds were deep, and the hatred seemed to have been distilled and intensified as it was passed down through the generations. I didn't know whether it would be possible, but I prayed that God would use me to dispel some of that hatred with the love of Christ. Perhaps that was one reason he had brought me there.

19

Rising Doubt

Not far from the church entrance, an old man lay sprawled, face down, on the pavement. It was a position that no one could be expected to assume willingly; the ground was covered not just by cigarette butts, but little globs of phlegm that had been hocked up and spit out by multitudes of crass shoppers. There was very likely a fair amount of urine, and possibly feces as well.

The man's clothes and face were covered in dirt, and he was missing more than a few teeth; but the most eye-catching thing about him was the way he shook. His head and his arms were in the grip of a steady tremor—perhaps even a seizure. Beside him on the pavement, inches from his face, was a cup containing spare change, revealing that he had initially come here to beg.

Most of the people who stood waiting in line to enter the church simply ignored him. But a young foreign woman who had just arrived—a brunette who was perhaps in her late twenties—rushed to kneel beside him. She removed a bottle from her purse, unscrewed the cap, and sprinkled some water onto the trembling beggar's mouth. It had no effect that any of us could see. While she tended to him, a passerby paused and stooped to place a one-kuai bill into the man's cup.

"No!" shouted the young woman. "He needs food and water!"

Her voice was filled with agonized compassion, and she was determined to get the old beggar the help he needed. She rummaged around in her purse for something edible, and after she fished out a plastic-wrapped snack, she alternated between trying to open it and shooing away people who wanted to drop change into the beggar's cup.

"He needs water, not money!" she shouted again.

I was moved by the girl's compassion, but I nevertheless felt the urge to laugh. The previous week, just before church, the same beggar had been in the same spot, shaking in exactly the same way—as he had been doing every Sunday for as long as I had been in China—when the police had shown up. As soon as he had spotted them, he had leapt up in mid-tremble, snatched his cup, and darted away with the agility of an Olympic gymnast.

There had been officers at either end of the street, however, and when he saw that he was surrounded, he surrendered to them with a good-natured, self-deprecating smile on his face. I had not been expecting him to take his act up so soon after the incident, but here he was again; and now, in the name of Christian compassion, this unwitting girl was ruining his business.

She would learn, though, just as I had learned.

When I had first arrived in China, I gave money to every beggar I saw. I knew that some might just spend the money on alcohol; but that was between them and God. Whether I gave to them or not, however, was between *me* and God—and that was the part of the equation for which I was responsible.

"Whatever you did for the least of these," Jesus would say on the day of judgment, "you did for me." Salvation was based on faith, but somehow the separation of the sheep and the goats would depend on a record of actions as well—actions that demonstrated a *living* faith. And so, not wanting to be a goat, I gave; but it didn't take long for my thinking to change.

The revelation had come as I was walking home from a restaurant. There was a stooped old beggar hobbling along in front of me, leaning heavily on a walking stick, limping so severely that it pained me just to watch him. *When I catch up to him*, I thought, *I'll give him some money.* As I drew nearer, the man reached the end of the block and rounded a corner. I followed him, fishing my wallet out of my pocket.

What I saw next, however, changed my mind.

Evidently, the beggar had considered his shift to be over as soon as he rounded that last corner; for when he did so, he stood up straight, swung his cane up over his shoulder, and picked up his pace, walking with a cheerful spring in his now limp-free step. The stoop and the limp had been nothing but an act; and I was suddenly left wondering how many of the beggars I saw regularly were *really* crippled.

Some time later, a foreign reporter published a series of stories about beggars in Beijing. It turned out that many of the beggars earned sizable middle-class incomes and lived in nice houses with big, happy families; and those weren't the truly evil ones. There were others who kidnapped and enslaved children in massive begging operations. They would deliberately remove the kids' limbs or burn their faces in order to intensify the visual and emotional impact on generous passersby.

There was something else about beggars that bothered me, though, something apart from their deception that chipped away disturbingly at my faith. It had to do with the ones who really *were* crippled—the ones with missing limbs, and the ones whose faces and arms were covered with grotesque burn scars. They were the ones who needed help most, even if— *especially* if—they were part of a crime ring.

What bothered me was that I couldn't do anything for them; and evidently no other Christian in Beijing could either. Had Jesus not healed paralytics? Had he not restored a severed ear, even? Had his disciples not gone out and healed people who were on their deathbeds? And were we not supposed to be empowered by the Holy Spirit to do "greater things than these"?

Believers were supposed to be filled with the Holy Spirit,

and he—the Spirit was a person (male, of course), not a thing—was supposed to give each of us gifts of power: prophecy, healing, speaking in tongues, and more. That ought to mean that any believing Christian—or at least *some* believing Christians—would have the power to heal the sick and even raise the dead.

And so I had tried it. When giving money to beggars with missing limbs or burned faces, I would place a hand on the beggar's shoulder or back. "Be healed, in the name of Jesus," I would say. But nothing happened. The very name of Jesus was supposed to be powerful; but where was that power? I had never seen it.

On an even more basic level, I couldn't help but notice that it wasn't just my grandiose prayers for miraculous healing that were frustratingly ineffective. My prayers for my students were bearing no fruit that I could see, either. My smaller requests seemed to be answered in random ways at best—ways that matched up suspiciously well with how things would work out in a godless world ruled by chance and the laws of nature alone.

Why did prayer not seem to work?

There were answers to this disturbing question, of course—different answers given by different people. Regarding the more ambitious prayers, some people said that the miraculous healing acts of the Holy Spirit had been part of a previous "dispensation" and were therefore not a part of God's plan for the present age; others said that you simply had to have enough faith.

Regarding prayer in general, it was said that you had to be sincere and persistent. You must be submissive, praying for God's will to be done. I did all of these things to the best of my ability, and I recognized that even though I was imperfect—and hence my faith was imperfect—God could quite easily use me nonetheless. According to the Bible, even if my faith was as small as a mustard seed, I should still have been able to move mountains.

And yet, even though I had been praying for all of my students by name—every student I'd ever had, past and present—not one had come to Christ. At best, they had acknowledged that Christianity was an element of foreign culture that ought to be respected. But that kind of acknowledgement could surely have been expected even without my prayers.

No, it was becoming painfully obvious that God simply did not answer my prayers with any kind of regularity that could be distinguished from randomness. The only available explanation was that God's ways were mysterious—and that in order to hide himself from nonbelievers and to maintain the requirement that even the most devoted believers proceed on faith alone, he always disguised his deeds so cleverly that they were indistinguishable from the course of nature.

How convenient.

I was beginning to feel that Christians who reasoned thus were simply making excuses for God. We were tying our minds in knots to perform the mental gymnastics required to maintain the plausibility of the existence of the omnipotent, beneficent deity described in the Bible despite an utter lack of evidence.

There was one other possibility, though, and I was eager to give it a chance. That possibility was that the full power of the Holy Spirit was indeed available to believers, but as the Pentecostals believed, it required something beyond being born again. It required a spiritual baptism, which I had perhaps not yet received. I knew where to go, though, if I wanted it: Matthew and Warren, the guys I'd met over the summer while training the next crop of ESI teachers.

They had been placed in Beijing at Sinopec, and they had offered to lay their hands on me and pray for me to receive the baptism of the Spirit. So I invited them over to my apartment to do so. There was nothing grand about it. I sat on my couch, and they stood behind me, each with a hand on one of my shoulders. I closed my eyes and bowed my head, and a moment later, they were both praying in tongues while I prayed silently and waited for God to move.

The intonations emerging from Matthew's mouth sounded to my ears like toddler babble. It was hard to believe that there might be any actual distinct words in what he was saying. The language Warren was speaking, on the other hand, sounded like a cross between the words of Greedo in *Star Wars* and a Latin Benedictine chant.

I opened my mouth, silently asking God to move my lips and give me the words to speak to his Spirit directly. In my mind, I surrendered myself to him as best I knew how. But I was resolved to wait for him to move my tongue; I wasn't going to try to force it on my own. I had heard of other people who had been given instructions to utter certain snatches of words and syllables in order to "get things started." But that sounded fake to me.

After perhaps fifteen minutes, Matthew and Warren finished praying, and then we talked for a while. I told them that I hadn't felt anything, but they assured me that the Spirit would begin moving within me soon. I just had to keep praying. And if, at some point, I opened my mouth and strange sounds came out, then I would know for sure that the Holy Spirit had filled me.

"If there's just one thing I can convince you of," Warren said, "it's that this is real. The Holy Spirit is real, and speaking in tongues is real." He seemed especially concerned with forfending against any suggestion that speaking in tongues was all just a big sham. Had he seen something in my expression that suggested I thought he was faking it? Perhaps he was just so used to people telling him it was fake that he felt the need to address what he saw as the most common objection.

Or was he trying to convince himself?

I wasn't intentionally being skeptical, though, and I didn't doubt that he and Matthew were sincere. Even if the sounds they made didn't resemble a "real" language to me, who was I to say that they didn't belong to some spiritual tongue that was beyond the discernment of a human ear? I was resolved to keep an open mind.

Weeks passed, and I continued praying for the anointing of the Holy Spirit. But I never felt anything. I opened my mouth and invited God to send the Spirit to move my lips for me, but nothing happened. I continued hoping that eventually the Spirit would take hold of me and I would receive the gift. But deep down, I slowly began to suspect that—for the obvious reason, which was that there *was* no Holy Spirit—I was bound to remain disappointed.

Still, I wanted to believe, and I asked God to help me overcome my doubts. I found myself clinging to Mark 9:24, in which the father of a sick boy begs Jesus to help him overcome his unbelief. If God had listened to him, surely he would do the same for me. All I had to do was keep praying and wait. But already I was growing weary.

20

Meet the Parents

The October holiday—China's National Day—was fast approaching. Leila and I had now been dating officially for almost a month, and her parents had decided that the holiday would be an appropriate time to invite me to their hometown of Dagang, in Tianjin.

"Guess what my mom asked about you?" Leila said.

I had no idea what it could be. Leila sounded excited, though, so it must have been something positive. She had told me that she and her mother talked to each other like friends, so I tried to imagine what two girls might say to each other about a boy. It had to be something about how our relationship was progressing, such as whether we had reached an important milestone. But surely no mother would ask her daughter, "Have you reached third base yet?"

"I don't know," I said.

"She asked what kind of food you like to eat!" she said. "She wants to know what she should cook for you."

"Oh." I said. "Anything is fine."

As the day approached, Leila told me that her parents had decided to cook jumbo shrimp, which were regarded as a delicacy in her hometown. She also told me that her dad was really looking forward to meeting her daughter's boyfriend, and he was especially excited about the fact that I was a foreigner. He had been telling his friends, and already several people had accused him of being stoked simply because he thought he could get something out of having an American son-in-law.

I was, of course, nervous about meeting her parents. Leila tried to put me at ease, telling me that they were good people. Her mother was a sales clerk in a pharmacy, and her father, having retired early from his work on an oil rig due to a back injury, had become a taxi driver. He was a practical man who, after once hitting a dog with his car, had taken its corpse home to make a stew out of it.

The holiday arrived, and we took a train to Tianjin. On the way there, I thought about some things that I should be prepared to say to Leila's parents. I would need to tell them my salary, and I had to be sure that I was using the proper forms of address.

"When my dad meets us at the train station, you have to say, 'Shushu hao,'" Leila told me. It meant basically, "Hello,

Uncle." That would be easy enough. I was to call her father *Shushu*, which meant "uncle," and her mother *Ayi*, which meant "aunt." It felt awkward for me, since in America I had never called *anyone* aunt or uncle. But I would have to internalize the words and get used to thinking of them as Shushu and Ayi—until Leila and I got married.

At last, we arrived at the Tianjin train station, and Leila spotted her father in the crowed and pointed him out to me. Shushu was short and slightly stout, with thick, spiky hair and sun-darkened skin. Most importantly, he was smiling when he saw us. He greeted me, took our bags, and led us to his car.

It was still about an hour and a half drive to Leila's home town, and on the way, I tried to make conversation with Shushu, but I was having trouble thinking of appropriate things to say. Fortunately, Leila had plenty to talk about with him, so there wasn't a whole lot of pressure.

Ayi also greeted me with a smile when we walked in the door. Their home was typical, with two bedrooms, a living room, a bathroom, and a kitchen. The dining table was essentially a card table, and as soon as we had taken our shoes off and put our luggage down, I was ushered over to it. We sat down and began eating immediately, and I was grateful to have something to put in my mouth because that meant I didn't have to talk.

I surveyed the food Ayi had prepared. There was a big plate of jumbo shrimp, a succulent-looking fish dish, some tofu, and several vegetable dishes. The sauce on the shrimp was very similar to American barbecue sauce, and it tasted quite good. The only complication was that I was unaccustomed to peeling shrimp. As a result, I was having an embarrassingly difficult time.

Ayi saw me struggling and asked how I liked the shrimp. I remembered how much Leila had said this kind of shrimp cost, so it was important that I only say good things about them. And they did taste good, so there shouldn't have been a problem.

"They're very good," I said in Chinese. Then I tried to say, "They're just difficult to eat."

Ayi's eyes widened, and she glanced at Leila in confusion. Leila rushed to explain in Chinese, and I heard her say, "He means they're not easy to eat."

"Oh," Ayi said.

It turns out that if you translate "difficult to eat" literally into Chinese, you get something that essentially means "disgusting." So I had just told my girlfriend's mother that her prized jumbo shrimp, the one thing she had been thinking about in advance and hoping to impress me with, tasted awful—within mere minutes after arriving in her home and sitting down at her kitchen table.

After the meal, Leila's parents ushered me into their living room, and we sat down to talk. Nothing could have prepared me for how quickly they went to the central issue: namely, the fact that I was dating their daughter. Ayi spoke first, and Leila translated the parts that I couldn't understand on my own, which turned out to be most of them.

"When I first heard that my daughter was seeing a

foreigner," she said, "I was unable to sleep for weeks. I was afraid that if she went to America, she would have a very hard life there." She paused and then said, "You must let her come visit us once a year."

Shushu asked me what kind of work I did, and I told him—I was a teacher and an editor. He asked how much money I made, and I told him that as well—5,500 kuai per month, not including the cost of my housing, which was provided for free. It was still a pittance by American standards, but significantly more than I'd made at Sinopec. Neither of her parents' faces gave away whether they thought it was a lot or a little.

"I want you to know," Shushu said, "that our daughter is worthless when it comes to housework. Do you understand?"

I turned to Leila, who looked somewhat embarrassed.

"He's saying that because he doesn't want you to treat me like a servant," she said.

I turned back to her father and said that I understood.

The conversation lasted somewhere between thirty minutes and an hour, and it peaked with Leila's father saying that he needed to know whether he could trust me. I stared at him blankly for a while, wondering what on earth I could do to earn his trust. Trustworthiness was something that could only be demonstrated over time, I felt. But he was staring at me, waiting for me to say something.

I looked at Leila.

"Tell him he can trust you," she said simply.

"You can trust me," I said.

Both of her parents nodded as if that had settled everything. They seemed to relax a little as soon as the words had come out of my mouth. I was shocked to see that those simple words were all they wanted. I had never before seen so much weight placed on words alone, and I felt a strong desire to go beyond my words to prove myself. Perhaps that was what they were depending on.

Shushu patted my leg and looked me in the eye. "Don't let me down," he said.

"I won't," I answered.

After only a short pause, Ayi looked at Leila. "We need to start planning the wedding, then," she said.

Leila had told me that in China, when a girl brings a significant other home to meet her parents, it's a huge step in their relationship. But I had no idea that marriage would be discussed within the first few hours.

We stayed with her parents for nearly the entire week. To make room for me, Shushu slept on the floor in the living room so that Leila could sleep with her mother, and I could have Leila's bedroom. I told them that I would have gladly slept on the floor, but they wouldn't hear any of it. I was the guest.

Over that holiday, I met more than just Leila's parents. She had uncles and aunts, as well as a few cousins that I had to meet. Since it was a holiday, they would be going out to eat together anyway, and I went with them. Two of Ayi's siblings were there: Leila's uncle, whom I·was to call *Lao Jiu*, and her aunt, whom I was to call *Lao Yi*. Their spouses and children were there was well. Lao Jiu's son, who was about seven, was fascinated with my arm hair, and after rubbing my arm for a second, said to his father, "Dad, can you grow arm hair like this?"

There was another man there, a family friend named "Uncle Lin." He was the owner of the pharmacy where Leila's mom worked, so it was especially important to maintain a good relationship with him. When he talked to me, I couldn't tell whether he was teasing me good-naturedly or trying to antagonize me maliciously. He asked me a question early on in the meal, and after processing his words for a moment, I decided that I actually understood what they meant: "What do you think of China's parks?"

"I think they're very nice," I replied.

Uncle Lin laughed and proceeded to talk more about the parks, but I very quickly lost track of what he was saying. Little words here and there stood out, and I thought I was occasionally able to piece together the meaning of a sentence or two. He said that China's parks were some of the worst in the world. They were very corrupt.

I asked Leila for some clarification, and it turned out that Uncle Lin had never been talking about parks in the first place. I had thought he was saying *gong yuan*, but he had actually been saying *gong wu yuan*. The "wu" was squashed and glossed over in the middle, so I just didn't hear it. And that made all the difference in the world, because *gong wu yuan* means "public servant," not "park." Uncle Lin had been talking about the rampant corruption among Chinese politicians.

The next topic that Uncle Lin took up seemed to make even less sense, and I was certain that I had misunderstood something. He began talking about America, and for some reason, he focused specifically on thermoses that were made in America. He said that America didn't have the technology to make decent thermoses. At least, that's what I thought he was saying.

I checked with Leila, and it turned out that I had understood correctly. China was far more advanced than America when it came to thermos technology. It seemed like a ridiculous thing to say, and in my mind I was formulating a catastrophically ill-advised response suggesting that however impressive China's thermos technology was, it still lagged somewhat behind America's space shuttle technology.

But before I could say anything, Lao Jiu—Leila's real uncle—finally interrupted Uncle Lin and said there was no point disparaging America's thermos technology. Every country, he said, had its advantages and disadvantages. After that, Uncle Lin finally stopped talking about America, and I was very grateful for Lao Jiu's diplomacy.

Finally, near the end of the meal, Uncle Lin again began talking to me, and this time I was sure that I didn't understand what he was saying. There was a particular word that kept coming up, which I didn't recognize: *cuoban*. It sounded like he was recommending a form of exercise to me. "It's very good for you!" he said. "Every day, kneel on a *cuoban* for one hour. You'll be amazed at how good it makes you feel. Go get one as soon as you can."

Once again, I checked with Leila. *Cuoban* meant "washboard," which in China would be a wooden board with deep, narrow grooves on it. It was a common form of punishment to make a disobedient child kneel on a washboard for a given amount of time. Uncle Lin was making sport of me. Still, I didn't really care, and I just wanted to be friendly. So I thought I would go along with his joke. "Wow, thanks for the advice! I'll go and get one immediately!" I said. But the fact that I was joking seemed to be lost on everyone.

Leila elbowed me, and under her breath, she whispered, "And give it to you." She was feeding me a line.

"And give it to you!" I added, loud enough for everyone to hear clearly.

Everyone but Uncle Lin burst out laughing. With Leila's help, I had finally come out on top after all the time Uncle Lin spent teasing me. Lao Jiu raised his glass to me, and I drank some beer with him.

After the meal, Uncle Lin declared that he was going to take us all out to a karaoke bar. I was a little worried, but the whole family was together, and with the women and children present, it couldn't end up like my trip to the Hollywood Club. So we went, and I sang a song that Leila had been teaching me. I looked around at the others in the room during a break in the song, expecting everyone to be impressed. But Uncle Lin had passed out on the couch, and the others were all talking. Leila was watching me, though, and she looked proud.

My visit to Tianjin was over before I knew it, and we were soon on a train back to Beijing. I used the time on the ride to compose a letter to Leila's parents, thanking them for their hospitality and assuring them once more that I would treat their daughter well. A week after I sent it, I got their reply. It was mostly reassuring but had a hint of sternness in it. They wanted to ensure that I would take good care of Leila.

I also decided that I should get to know Leila's younger brother, Ben, who was still in college. I got his email address from Leila and wrote him a message in Chinese, introducing myself and expressing a desire to get to know him. The first line of his reply was a bit shocking: He used the respectful term of address for "brother-in-law" (*jiefu*). Apparently I wouldn't have any trouble garnering acceptance from him.

It now seemed that I had secured everyone's approval. Apart from Uncle Lin, who wasn't really part of the family, they had all been very kind to me. And evidently, plans for a wedding were already underway. We had only to pick a date.

21

In Pursuit of Stardom

Reluctantly, I unzipped my pants and showed the old man my penis. With undisguised delight, he stared for an uncomfortable amount of time—well, any amount of time would have been uncomfortable—before giving me a big thumbs-up and shouting, "GOOD!" I was both relieved and disappointed that he didn't bother to feel my testicles.

The previous week, the Semiconductor Institute had announced that it would be providing free medical exams for all students and faculty. It was an all-day affair in which everyone—five hundred or so people—went to a particular building and stood in line forever at each of a dozen small rooms where a doctor did some test or other.

At first I didn't want to go. I was a bit skeptical of Chinese doctors, and I didn't know whether I would be able to understand anything they might say about my health anyway. Perhaps most importantly, I was the only foreigner at the whole school, and I really didn't want to be a spectacle. But one of my coworkers convinced me I had nothing to lose and that if I *did* have a problem, the doctors would find it.

So I went.

The first thing I had to do was get a urine cup at the entrance, stand in line at the bathroom, fill the cup, and then set it on a towering cart loaded with hundreds of other urine cups. That part was easy and went off without a hitch; but things got awkward when I got to the rooms where medical personnel actually had to examine me.

At the ultrasound station, where they were apparently checking various internal organs, the technicians started arguing about whether the machine would work on a foreigner, and if it did, whether or not they should be looking for the same things in my organs that they looked for in Chinese people's organs. In the end, they decided to treat me just as they would have treated a Chinese patient.

The technicians at the next station saw something in my EKG that they didn't like and sent me over to an old man sitting at a desk. He looked at the printout, frowned, and then started talking. I couldn't understand a word he said. His voice wasn't clear, he had a local accent, and he was using a bunch of medical terms. Finally, he scrawled a few characters on my chart and handed it back to me. Wanting to know what he thought was wrong with my heart, I went to several of my native colleagues and asked them to tell me what the old man had written; but no one could decipher it.

From there, I moved on and got a chest X-ray; I had blood drawn; I waited in line for ten minutes to see a gynecologist before someone told me what the line was for; and then at the next station, there was a doctor sitting at a desk in the middle of the room. There was no equipment that I could see. The doctor just looked at me with a combination of uncertainty and expectation.

"Um . . . What are you checking here?" I asked.

"Nothing," she said. "I'm just here to answer any questions you might have. This is the consultation room."

"Oh," I said.

"Do you have any questions?"

"No."

The only station I hadn't been to yet was the "men's medicine" station, where people were evidently being screened for testicular cancer or hernias. Never one to enjoy a testicle exam, I had been considering skipping it; but my coworker's words kept playing in my mind: "If you *do* have a problem, the doctors will find it." So I got in line.

The doctor was a stooped, snowy-haired old man who giggled with glee when he saw that I was a foreigner. To my surprise, he spoke to me in English. "Hello, foreigner!" he said.

"Hi," I replied.

He giggled again and then proceeded to question me, clearly delighted to be using English—perhaps for the first time in his career. "Nose?" he said, pointing at my face.

"Nose," I repeated, wondering what on earth he was doing. He hadn't checked any of the other men's noses that I had seen.

He nodded, looking at me expectantly. "Your nose?"

"My nose?" I asked. "My nose is good."

"GOOD!" he said. "Mouth?"

"Good," I said.

"GOOD!" he slapped his knee and giggled. "Heart?"

"Good."

"GOOD!" More giggling. "Lungs?"

"Good."

"GOOD!"

Then there was a pause. He was looking at me, trying to remember something. I glanced behind me. There were about twenty men in line waiting to be examined, and the old doctor was just practicing his English with me.

"PENIS!" he suddenly yelled.

"Good," I answered again, still following the established pattern. At this point, I just wanted to be done with the encounter; but a verbal response apparently wasn't enough for the old man. He motioned for me to unzip my pants, and I did so.

The examination didn't take long, and once he had declared that my penis was good, I slipped away quietly, avoiding eye contact with the other guys waiting in line—some of whom were my students—and retreated to my apartment.

I had been warned that as a foreigner in China, I would be the object of much fascination. Usually, this meant nothing more than being stared at in the marketplace or being approached by curious strangers. Now I knew that it also meant having my penis examined with a disturbing degree of enthusiasm. And I was about to learn that it might even make it possible for me to become a pop star.

Shows like American Idol were immensely popular at the time, and there were tons of derivative programs in China, the most prominent one being *Super Girl*. Every school, from elementary through university, seemed to have caught the talent show fever—including the Semiconductor Institute. Each year, there was a karaoke contest that was judged by local professional musicians and had two separate rounds, with a two-week interim to allow the finalists time to prepare a second performance.

My students urged me to enter the contest, and I acquiesced, thinking that it would be a good opportunity to practice my Chinese and engage with the community. So I set about learning one of Leila's favorite songs, the theme song for the Hong Kong movie *Wu Jian Dao* (the film from which Martin Scorsese's *The Departed* was copied).

I made it to the second round, learned another song, and ended up finishing in second place. My students and colleagues were so enthusiastic about my ability to sing in Chinese that one of them signed me up to compete on the wildly popular show *Foreigners Sing Chinese Songs*. It was a show that targeted Chinese people's obsession with watching foreigners speak Chinese—something that provided guaranteed entertainment, since white people speaking crappy Chinese was hilarious, while white people speaking good Chinese was amazing.

As I advanced through the rounds, it really did begin to seem possible that I might become a star. My students told me that I could be the next *Da Shan*—the most recognized foreigner in China, a Canadian who was paid millions just to host TV shows. And when the TV station called me up to say they were so impressed with my Chinese that they wanted me to come in and make an appearance on another show, I began to dream of stardom.

I showed up at the studio on the appointed day, figuring that I would probably play someone's eccentric foreign neighbor who would say some embarrassing things. No big deal. But it turned out that they wanted me to be on a celebrity game show. There were three local celebrities that I didn't recognize, and I was going to compete with them in various party games. It was not going to be fair at all.

The first game actually didn't go too badly, because it was a singing game, and they let me pick the song I wanted to sing. I chose the recent hit "Two Butterflies," and a guy started playing the accompaniment on a keyboard. I began singing, and then he changed keys. And then tempo. And style. He started going faster and faster, and higher and higher, until my voice failed. That was the point of the game—to see who could last the longest.

Next was a word game. They put cards on our foreheads with words written on them in Chinese. Each player could see everyone else's word but not his own, and the goal was to try to trick other players into saying the words on their cards. Behind us, at the back of the stage, stood two hulky guys, one wearing a giant black bear costume, and the other dressed as a stegosaurus. I wondered what their role was.

The game started before I even understood the instructions, and the three celebrities converged on me. Before I knew what was happening, I had said the word on my card. And then I found out what the bear and the stegosaurus were for. They came up behind me, grabbed my arms, and dragged me to the back of the stage, where they then popped a giant, confetti-filled balloon over my head—the penalty for saying the word on my card.

After the first round, they replaced everyone's cards and started over. Once again, the celebrities converged on me. And then again. And again. After four balloons had been popped over my head, the director yelled "cut" and shouted that he didn't want the whole game to consist of embarrassing the foreigner repeatedly. They focused on each other after that, and I tried to participate; but my Chinese just wasn't good enough.

When they aired the show, I was just a foreign idiot standing on the sidelines with a brainless grin on his face. I felt betrayed. I would have been able to deliver scripted lines just fine. But the kind of quick thinking and witty banter that were required for that show were beyond my Chinese level. If I was going to become a star, I would have to appear on a different type of show.

A chance to redeem myself came just a few weeks later,

when I got another phone call from a lady at the studio. "We're doing a program on *xinliyisheng*," she said, "and we'd like to interview some foreigners on TV. People in China aren't very familiar with *xinliyisheng*, so we're trying to promote understanding of it."

I thought about what she was saying. The word *xinliyisheng* sounded familiar, but I couldn't remember exactly where I'd heard it before. I recognized the characters in it, and I thought about their literal translation: "heart management doctor." At that moment, it seemed obvious to me that it had to mean "cardiologist." Promoting a better understanding of cardiology sounded noble, so I agreed to participate.

"Great!" she said. "I just want to ask you some preliminary questions. If you have experience and have anything to say, then we'll invite you to the studio for an interview."

I thought back to the frightening experience I'd had with palpitations in sixth grade. Since then, I had seen a cardiologist several times. I figured I'd have a lot to say, and I was feeling good about the interview. Finally, I was going to have something intelligent and helpful to say on TV.

"Have you ever used the services of a *xinliyisheng*?" the lady asked.

"Yes."

"When?"

"Well, the first time was when I was in middle school. I think I was eleven years old." As I spoke, I imagined that the lady must be smiling at the other end of the line. Yes, I was going to be a gold mine on cardiology.

"Can you tell me something about your condition?"

"One day just after gym class, when I was in sixth grade, my heart started beating in a strange way."

"Oh," the interviewer said. "So you went to see a *xinli-yisheng*?"

"Well, yeah. I guess it seemed like the obvious thing to do. I found out that my dad also had a heart condition, and he'd been to see a *xinliyisheng* and gotten some medication. So they made an appointment and took me to see one too."

"And the *xinliyisheng* was able to help you?"

"Yes. He told me to drink less caffeine. And it worked. My heart stopped bothering me."

After that, the lady thanked me, and the interview was over. Something about the whole thing bothered me, though, and I picked up my dictionary to look up the word *xinli-yisheng*. I saw that it didn't mean "cardiologist" after all. It meant "psychologist."

The studio didn't call me again after that.

I couldn't help thinking that things might have turned out differently if they had only given me a different kind of show to be on. I told myself that the end of my TV career— not that it had even come close to becoming a career—was a *good* thing. I hadn't come to China in search of fame and fortune, after all, but to share the Gospel. And as an extreme introvert, I wasn't cut out to be a celebrity. But it was a nice fantasy while it lasted.

22

A Cat and a Ring

I slurped the last drop of broth from my bowl and scanned the other remaining patrons in the California Beef Noodle King. Across the room from me sat a man who was eating by himself. I caught him looking at me, and he dropped his eyes. I had long since grown accustomed to being stared at; but prying eyes were beginning to seem like a much greater threat now.

Half an hour earlier, I had been leading a men's Bible study at Haidian Church. Nominally, it was a weekly English lesson for the men on the translation team; but in fact, the English lessons had long ago turned into theology lessons. I was the teacher, despite my utter lack of formal qualifications. In the evangelical community, the only prerequisites for teaching theology seemed to be faith and familiarity with the Bible—and a man's share of testosterone.

The Chinese government didn't like foreigners coming over and indoctrinating their citizens, though. Religious ideologies in particular, with any sort of emphasis on an Authority that was higher than the Communist Party, were seen as especially threatening. I could be kicked out of the country for what I was doing. In the past, this possibility hadn't really bothered me; but now that it would mean permanent separation from Leila, I was afraid.

When I left the restaurant, I glanced over my shoulder to make sure I wasn't being followed. My fears were overblown, of course. In reality, the government had much better things to do with its time than to keep an eye on a lone teacher in Beijing who was just meeting with a handful of guys once a week. But still, I *did* know of people who had been kicked out. Was I *really* just being paranoid? This was an argument that I was beginning to have with myself nearly every day.

On my way home, I resolved to reduce my ministry activities. It wouldn't be fair to Leila to endanger our relationship. Our future together meant everything to me. In her family's eyes, we were betrothed, and in a few months, I was planning to take her back to America to attend my brother's wedding as my fiancée. The only thing we lacked at the moment was a ring—and obtaining one was at the top of my "to do" list.

Thinking about buying a diamond ring was a big source of stress. I hated shopping in China because I wasn't good at bargaining. I imagined that I would go to some jewelry store and end up being sold a piece of glass for two thousand dollars. To avoid such an outcome, I enlisted the help of a former student, a guy who went by the English name Biff.

Biff took me to a department store, and he waited patiently while I looked at all kinds of diamond rings. When I found the one I liked, it was love at first sight. Once I had paid for it and we were leaving the store, I had a huge smile on my face. I was raving about how perfect I thought the ring was, and I kept thanking Biff for helping me. He chuckled with amusement.

"I remember when I picked out my wife's engagement ring," he said. His eyes glazed over as he stared into the past. "I had such high expectations for our marriage." Then he went silent, and his features settled into a look of resignation.

Well, I thought, whatever happened to Biff's marriage won't happen to mine.

I had long ago settled on the perfect way to give Leila the ring. I would have one of our favorite photographs—a picture of us in the middle of a park with the sun setting over our heads—turned into a jigsaw puzzle, and I would print the words, "Will you marry me?" on the back. After an evening out, we would assemble the puzzle together, and I would turn it over to reveal the question. Then I would bring the ring out.

I found a company that made jigsaw puzzles and placed an order. When the box arrived a few weeks later, I could barely contain my excitement. But upon opening it, I saw that they had changed the color of the photograph. It was all in shades of pink now. And it was covered with glitter, too. Some designer at the company had probably thought they were doing me a favor by spicing it up; but it was awful.

I needed a Plan B.

I tried to think of all the things that Leila liked. The first thing that came to mind was her favorite childhood cartoon character, whose Chinese name translates to English as "Machine Cat." He was a blue robotic cat who was afraid of mice. Leila loved everything about him. His most interesting feature was a pocket on his belly that contained all sorts of magical items. "I wish I had a magic pocket like Machine Cat's," she would frequently say. When I remembered that, it was obvious what I should do: give her a stuffed Machine Cat with the ring hidden in his pocket.

I decided to do it on her birthday. She had the day off, and I knew that she was going to come over to my apartment while I was still at work, so I set everything up for her to find when she arrived. I put the ring in an envelope, together with a love letter, and placed it in Machine Cat's pocket. Then I placed the cat on the coffee table and covered it with a colorful box. For the finishing touch, I set a recording of "Happy Birthday" playing on a loop. Then I sent Leila a message asking her not to look inside the box until I got home.

When she arrived, she circled the coffee table, staring at the box and wondering what was in it—but she didn't open it. I got home and further tortured her by insisting that we go out to dinner first. Only when we got back did I finally let her lift the box. With a delighted squeal at the sight of Machine

Cat, she picked him up and hugged him. I gently suggested that she check his pocket.

Tears began streaming down her cheeks as soon as she saw the ring and the letter. And suddenly I wasn't sure what to do. It my first time proposing to a girl. The letter asked her to marry me, and she was already holding the ring. I worried that it might be redundant to kneel and voice the question aloud; but I decided to go ahead and do it anyway.

"Yes," she said, slipping the ring on. "Of course I'll marry you!"

Exactly one hundred days after we had officially begun dating, we were now engaged. There were some details to arrange, of course, and the bride price was one of them. If Leila or her parents had been the ones to tell me about it, I might have felt a little suspicious. But everybody—my students, the guys in my Bible study, my colleagues at the Semiconductor Institute—told me the same thing: I had to give Leila's parents some money.

"How much?" I asked several people.

"Maybe thirty thousand kuai," said one.

"It doesn't have to be money," said another. "I gave my in-laws a vase."

Finally, I asked Leila.

"I think twenty thousand should be enough," she said. "Let me check with my parents." She called them and confirmed that they would accept twenty thousand kuai in exchange for their daughter. So I went to the bank and withdrew it. Together, we went to Tianjin, and I handed the money over to her parents.

As her mother took the envelope, she said, "Actually, this money is not really for us. It's for Leila." Leila later explained that it was a sort of insurance policy. If they thought I wasn't doing a good enough job of taking care of her, they could use that money to help her out. Or, as was the most common custom at the time, the money could be used to furnish our new home.

After the money was handed over, her dad drove us all to the courthouse. I paid a fee of twenty-six kuai, and the official who worked there printed out and stamped two marriage certificates, one for each of us. We were now officially married— in the government's eyes, at least. But our actual wedding still had yet to be planned.

To most Chinese people, there was nothing ambiguous about our situation. It was perfectly ordinary to get married at a courthouse and then have a formal wedding banquet as much as a year later, when you were able to get both families together. To me, though, our status wasn't clear. Was it the legal document that mattered, or was there some spiritual bond that could only occur at a wedding ceremony, for which God wanted us to wait?

I reflected on what the Bible said about marriage. I remembered vaguely the story about Isaac taking Rebekah into his mother's tent and "marrying" her. To the ancient Hebrews—and therefore to God, I supposed—marriage consisted of three things: parental consent, an exchange of gifts, and a little bit of activity in a tent. Nevertheless, I felt that the church wedding ceremony was what really counted. And so, when we stayed with Leila's parents, we maintained the separate sleeping arrangements that we had used on my first visit.

"Why aren't you sleeping together?" Leila's father asked us.

It wasn't that he was encouraging us to have sex. Rather, he was eager to get out of sleeping on the living room floor. Leila explained our decision, and her parents nodded, though they clearly thought it bizarre.

The timing of our trip to the courthouse had been a matter of strategy. We weren't really in a hurry to get married, but I figured that having an official license would improve Leila's chance of receiving a visa. My brother's wedding was two months off yet, but the visa application process was rather long and complicated, and we wanted to do all we could to ensure success. So when it came time to attend her interview at the U.S. embassy, we brought an entire backpack full of documentation in addition to our marriage license.

The embassy was inside a walled compound, and we had to show my U.S. passport and Leila's invitation letter to get in. Once in, we queued up outside of the interview building. It was winter, and the ground was covered with snow. Our faces quickly grew numb in the freezing air. After two hours, Leila was at last ushered inside. But I had to wait out in the cold.

What was happening inside of the building was a mystery to me. I watched as people slowly trickled out while others filed in. The result of each person's interview was easy to discern. The people who came out with smiles on their faces had clearly been granted a visa; others emerged dismayed or outright angry, snapping at companions who had been waiting outside for them.

I stamped my feet and kept moving to try to stay warm, but the cold was growing more and more painful. I imagined that Leila was being interviewed at that moment, and I prayed for her. *God, please let them grant her a visa. Help her to explain everything clearly. Give her favor in the interviewer's eyes.* And then I added the conventional escape clause: *If it be your will.*

For three hours, I kept telling myself that Leila was going to emerge any minute. And then, just when I was beginning to worry seriously about frostbite, she came out at last. She was not smiling. When our eyes met, she shook her head.

So it had *not* been God's will.

After dinner that evening, Leila burst into tears.

Anger boiled inside me over the injustice of it all. In my view, the interviewer's job was to judge whether we were being honest—whether our relationship was genuine and whether Leila could be counted on to return to China after my brother's wedding. But he had apparently decided that we were lying. Why else would they not let her go with me?

As my brother's wedding date approached, I tried to comfort myself with theological arguments. Jesus had suffered a much greater injustice. He, the innocent Lamb, had been put to death for no crime at all—or rather, for *other* people's crimes—and he had suffered willingly. This experience was a lesson, I decided, to help me understand firsthand what it was like to be the victim of an injustice. God's purpose was for me to share in Christ's suffering and thereby know him better.

I was only going to be gone for ten days, but Leila was very distressed when I left. I would quite literally be on the other side of the world, and the denial of her visa had shown that our freedom to be together could be taken away at any time. China might just as easily deny me a visa in the future. And if neither of us could travel to the other's country, what would become of our relationship?

The thought gave both of us nightmares.

Those ten days passed quickly, though. While I was in America, Leila celebrated Spring Festival with her family in Tianjin. And when I returned to Beijing, she welcomed me just as she had when I came back at the end of the summer. My apartment was sparkling. She had tidied the rooms, mopped the floor, and taken out the trash. And dinner was on the table.

At the end of the evening, when it was the usual time for me to walk her to the bus stop, we looked at each other. We had just been on separate continents for ten days, and we didn't want to be apart again for another minute. And so, for the first time, she didn't go home at night. It was a change in plans; but we *were* married, and it seemed that there shouldn't have been anything wrong with it.

23

A Painful Separation

The phone rang, and I picked it up. It was Lillian, my former supervisor at ESI, with whom Leila and I were still friends. I immediately sensed that she was nervous, and I suspected that I knew why. As soon as the pleasantries were out of the way, my suspicion was confirmed.

"Are you and Leila living together?" she asked.

Until now, the spring semester had been proceeding normally for the most part. I had rebooted my courses at the Semiconductor Institute, I was still attending Haidian Church, and my weekly Bible studies with the men on the translation team had resumed. The biggest change was that Leila had indeed moved in with me.

It was a farcical question, really. What she meant was,

"Are you having sex?" I could easily have been annoyed, even angry, at the intrusiveness of it. But I wasn't. I understood Lillian's concern perfectly. In fact, I would likely have done the same thing had I been in her shoes. And I would have felt the same fear about how the conversation might go.

There were two possibilities. The first was that I could simply have said no; but Leila and I had not been hiding our status, and an outright denial would have constituted a bald-faced lie, a rejection of Lillian's right to express a sister's concern for our behavior. The second possibility was just as bad: I might admit it and then say, "So what?" If I did that, I would be cutting both Leila and myself off from our network of Christian brothers and sisters in Beijing. Either response was unthinkable.

"Yes," I said at last.

My honesty relieved some of the tension. I don't remember our exact words, but in the conversation that followed, Lillian made it clear that she considered it a mistake—a sin, really—for Leila and me to have moved in together. I defended our decision by pointing out that we were legally married; but I didn't blow Lillian off. Rather, I considered her perspective carefully.

I knew that Lillian would not have made that phone call without first consulting her most trusted Christian friends about whether Leila and I were in the wrong. Her intervention represented the disapproval of not just one woman, but likely an entire community. And that gave me pause. *Were* we sinning? If so, what should we do about it?

A non-Christian might ask why I cared at all. If Lillian was butting her nose into my relationship with Leila and foisting her interpretation of Christian morality upon us, why not simply tell her that it was none of her business? But such a thought would never have occurred to me. I believed in the importance of mutual correction within the body of Christ. And on a more personal level, Lillian was both a good person and a good friend. I recognized how difficult it must have been for her to make that phone call, and I respected her deeply for it.

As it turned out, I wasn't the only one who had received a call about the matter. Chanel, one of the translators at Haidian Church, had called Leila to ask the same question. Chanel was more distressed than Lillian, and she exhorted us directly to confess our sin and repent. Before long, a fairly extensive effort was underway to help Leila and me find our way back to the path of righteousness. Since I prided myself on being open to correction, I genuinely wanted to find out what God wanted us to do.

Lillian and her teammate, Sadie, were certain that my marriage to Leila would only be made real in God's eyes by a wedding ceremony in the church—not a government certificate. It wasn't so much that the ceremony had to be conducted by a pastor but that our union had to be witnessed by the body of Christ. I wasn't sure exactly where in the Bible that idea came from, but it seemed reasonable to me.

Chanel, meanwhile, consulted with a pastor at Haidian Church and then shared the pastor's response with us:

"Maybe they shouldn't have moved in together before the wedding ceremony. But the start of their new life together should be a joyful occasion, and they need the support of their brothers and sisters in the church. If they want me to do the ceremony for them just because you're pressuring them to do it, then I will refuse."

When I heard those words, I hoped that the matter was settled: The pastor had declared that everyone should support us. What could be clearer than that? Unfortunately for us, though, a large number of people seemed to think that "supporting" us meant pressuring us to stop living together.

I met with Gary for further counsel, and his input did not make me feel any better. It was clear to him, he said, that I had led Leila into sin. The only way forward would be for her to move out until our wedding day. "You can't live together," he said, "and then have Leila walk down the aisle in a white dress at your wedding."

The white dress symbolized purity—which meant virginity, of course. If Leila moved out and we repented of our sins, then she would once again become pure in God's eyes. Only then could she put on a wedding dress in good conscience, and we would all be free to pretend that nothing had ever been amiss.

"I guess it's partly my fault," Gary added. "You did ask me to hold you accountable, and I didn't make much effort to do that."

Matthew's response was very different from everyone else's. When I told him that Leila and I had been living together, he laughed. "I should have known! I've been coming over to your apartment, and every time I used your bathroom, there were all these girly things in the bathroom and all this long black hair in the shower. It just didn't occur to me!"

In response to the question of whether Leila and I were living in sin, he said, "I have no idea. Let me do some reading and praying, and I'll get back to you." He saw it as a puzzle to be solved and set off to carry out the Christian equivalent of a science experiment. With no preconceived notions, no ready response, and no gut feeling as to whether Leila and I were spiritually married, he was going to collect data to ascertain the answer via the guidance of the Holy Spirit and the scriptures.

A few days later, he got back to me by email. After combing through the Bible and reading various online theological articles about the nature of Christian marriage, he concluded that there was no reason to suppose that our marriage was not legitimate in God's eyes. "But," he added, "if you still want to go ahead and have a ceremony, I'd be happy to do it. Nobody here knows this about me, but I'm an ordained minister." It turned out that he had been ordained by his church when he was only fifteen.

I took comfort in Matthew's assessment. But it still didn't end the matter. For one thing, none of the other people who objected to our living together accepted his conclusion; and for another, I felt that there was more to the issue than I had shared with Matthew—or with anyone else, for that matter. What really troubled me was not the possibility that we might not be married in God's eyes, but rather that when we had gotten our marriage license in the first place, I had resolved that we would live separately until our church wedding. It was a resolution that I regarded as a promise to God—one that I had now broken.

The very fact that I had made such a resolution revealed a deep and perhaps subconscious conviction that I considered our church wedding to be the true beginning of our marriage. This conviction seemed to be confirmed by all of the others who thought we were living in sin, and it was beginning to tear me apart inside. Before long, I was unable to think about anything else.

A feedback loop had been triggered. My uncertainty suggested to me that I was probably wrong. "If you have to ask whether what you're doing is sinful, then it's probably sinful," was the way I tended to think. So it was beginning to seem more and more likely that I was not just in a gray area, but in blatant sin. This gave me an increasing sense of guilt, which further confirmed that I must have been living in sin.

After another day or two, I developed a fever. There were no other symptoms that I remember. It wasn't a cold or the flu. I had no runny nose, no sore throat, no cough, no intestinal issues. Just a fever. At first, it didn't seem like a big deal, and I went to bed expecting to feel better in the morning. But the next day, it was worse.

Leila went to work as usual, but I stayed home. I took a dose of a fever reducer that I'd gotten from a Chinese pharmacy a few months earlier. It had worked for me before, but this time it had no effect. I took my temperature every hour, and it was steadily rising. By noon, it was over 39 degrees Celsius, and it was inching up toward 40. I converted the numbers to Fahrenheit and realized that as far back as I could remember, I'd never had such a high fever before.

I took another dose of the fever reducer and waited for another hour, but my temperature didn't go down—not even by a fraction of a degree. When I saw that the medicine had no effect, I became certain that my fever was spiritual in origin. This was, as I saw it, the final confirmation that I was living in sin and needed to confess and repent. At this point, I didn't seem to have much time left. So I called Lillian.

"I need you to come over," I said.

She asked why, and I explained about the fever. A short time later, she arrived at my apartment, together with Sadie. I ushered them to the living room, where we all sat down. Almost as soon as I began talking, I was bawling like a child. I told them about what I now saw as my broken promise to God, and I asked for their help. I didn't know what to do. I didn't want to hurt Leila, but God had to come first.

"You're lucky," Sadie said. "A fever is a small punishment for breaking a promise to God." I nodded in agreement, and Sadie's judgment ended there. She and Lillian laid out a possible solution, and it sounded good to me—though again, I felt at the time that I had no choice. They would find Leila a place to stay, and we could live separately for the remaining month before our wedding. Everything would be all right. My relief was immeasurable.

Sadie prayed for me, and then she and Lillian left. My fever dropped over the next few hours. It was a powerful confirmation that I had indeed needed to repent. Furthermore, it bolstered my fragile faith: At that moment, no question about evolution or inconsistencies in the Bible could have bothered me. God had given me a fever, and he had taken it away. That was all the proof I needed that he was there. Not everything *had* to make sense to me.

A short time later, Lillian called to say that she had a friend who would let Leila live with her. Her name was Lucia. Everything was now lined up, and I had only to break the news to Leila when she got home from work. She had known that this was what our friends were pressuring us to do, but she was bound to be crushed nonetheless, especially since the final decision had been made without her.

Upon her arrival in the evening, I asked her to go for a walk with me. We bundled ourselves up in our down jackets to fend off the winter's cold, and as we walked along the sidewalk around the campus, I told her everything that had happened—and everything that had been decided. She would have to move out, and we would have to live separately until the wedding.

As I watched to see how she would respond, she turned away from me. I had to circle around her and look inside the hood of her jacket to see her face. What I saw twisted my heart. Her eyes were wells of pain. And anger. Without a word, she walked back toward our apartment. She didn't even look at me. I followed after her, calling out to her, but she might as well not have heard.

Back in our apartment—*my* apartment now—she began packing her bags, still without uttering a sound. It terrified me. Was she packing to move into Lucia's apartment—or to leave me? Perhaps in her mind, they were the same thing at the moment.

A short time later, Lillian and Sadie arrived with Lucia, and Leila left with them. I told her that I loved her, but the words sounded hollow to me, and at the moment I was sure that she didn't want to hear them. Once the door had closed behind her, I was left wondering whether there would ever even *be* a church wedding.

24

Purification

How do you win back the affection of a girl whose hatred you have thoroughly earned? If she won't even answer the phone, repeated calls would surely only drive her further away. Would an email apology work? An occasional text message affirming my continued love? Little messages wishing her good morning and good night—the sorts of texts that had kindled our love in the first place?

I could only hope.

In the meantime, with our new living arrangement, the time for my own purification had come. I had to get right with God—and over more than just my relationship with Leila. Other issues that needed to be addressed had been brought to my attention. One of them, according to Sadie, was the demonic presence in my apartment.

Over the past year, I had received various gifts from students and friends. Everyone tended to give me objects that were quintessential representations of some aspect of Chinese culture: carvings of the Buddha, dragons, and other fantastic creatures. One of the most egregious items in my possession was a set of Peking Opera masks, which were sitting in a frame on one of my bookshelves.

Since throwing out the little Jade Buddha that Bonnie had given me at Sinopec a year earlier, I had grown lax. Sadie reminded me that these were not harmless objects. They were images of gods or other spirits; and since they weren't the Christian God, they were demonic. To keep them in my home was to invite these demons to influence my life. Having just experienced the inexplicable fever that had faded only after my repentance, I was inclined to believe all of this. So I resolved to get rid of them.

Just as with the Jade Buddha, I felt that throwing the items in the trash wouldn't be enough; I had to break each object physically to ensure that they would harm no one else. I gathered up all of the precious gifts that my students and friends had given me out of love, and I carried them out to the courtyard late at night, when I was sure everyone else had gone to bed. I didn't want anyone to see me destroying these beautiful representations of Chinese culture.

It was cold, and a biting wind whipped about me as I worked. While shattering the clay masks, I imagined that the wind was a manifestation of the demonic spirits fighting against their destruction. It might have been a frightening thought, but I had God on my side. He would protect me from any retribution that these spirits might wish to exact upon me, especially now that I was purging my life of these idols that had been so displeasing to him.

In the following days, I spent hours reading my Bible and praying. I felt as if my faith had been rejuvenated. And best of all, Leila began talking to me again. We went on a date, and I was overwhelmed by relief that we were once again able to laugh over a meal and hold hands as we walked along the sidewalk. Our relationship was not ruined after all. At the end of the evening, I escorted her back to Lucia's apartment.

What I saw shocked me.

As soon as the taxi entered Lucia's neighborhood, I felt as if we had left Beijing. One of the things that I had always liked about Beijing was that it seemed that I could walk the streets at any time of night and not fear for my safety. Perhaps my pocket would be picked, but I had never once felt the possibility of a threat of violence, even when I was alone at midnight. But Lucia's neighborhood didn't give me that feeling.

It was little more than a shanty town. The "houses" were made of brick and plaster rather than the old wooden boards and corrugated aluminum that I'd seen in the true slums, but the feeling was the same. Lucia's complex consisted of a few rows of long, single-story buildings that were divided into individual rooms. The whole thing reminded me of a dilapidated self-storage facility.

The room Lucia called home had an area of perhaps one

hundred square feet. There was a mattress on the floor that filled nearly the entire space. Some makeshift shelves hung from the back wall. There was no kitchen, no closet or cabinet, and nothing that could be used as a countertop. There wasn't even a toilet. To go to the bathroom or take a shower, one would have to cross the dirt road to the public restroom, which could be smelled from Lucia's front door. The only amenities at all were a dirty old sink and a little space heater that sat on the floor in a corner.

At the sight of it all, I despised myself. It was my fault that Leila was living in this place. If her parents had known that I had landed her here, they would have wanted to throw me off a cliff. I wondered whether Lillian and Sadie had known what the conditions here were like before they suggested that Leila live with Lucia. I marveled that Leila was willing to endure it—for me.

And endure it she did.

The wedding was still on. In fact, we would be having two of them. The first would be our church wedding. It would take place on the Saturday before Easter—almost exactly a year after Gary had introduced us to each other in line at church. The second would be a more traditional Chinese banquet in Dagang, Leila's hometown, eight days later. In between, we would take a cruise on the Yangtze River.

Leila went out with Chanel to shop for a wedding dress. We printed and mailed invitations and reserved a block of rooms for friends and family at hotels in Beijing and Dagang. Then we booked a restaurant at the end of the promenade where the church was located and picked out the food for the reception.

As the big day approached, it became difficult to contain my excitement. My family and friends from America would be crossing the ocean to join us. Many of my students from both Sinopec and the Semiconductor Institute were planning to attend as well, and my former colleagues from ESI would also come to celebrate with us. But best of all, I would soon be able to live with my wife once more.

When the day arrived at last, everybody converged on Haidian Church at 10:30 in the morning. The fact that I was a foreigner made it a popular wedding to attend. People we didn't know—people who weren't even members of the church—walked in off the street and sat down in the back to watch. At the time, the church was still meeting in an old restaurant on the dingy Haidian Book Town promenade. There were no pews, and ordinarily there was no aisle for a bride to walk down. So early in the morning, the church staff had rearranged the chairs and rolled out a red carpet to make an aisle.

As groom, I stood in the middle of the sanctuary just before the small platform from which the pastors normally preached their sermons. The senior pastor, Pastor Wu, stood with me on the floor rather than on the platform, using a music stand to hold his papers. The ceremony began with a hymn sung by the choir, and it warmed my heart to see the other pastors standing among them, singing with broad smiles on their faces.

There was no foyer or separate room of any sort in which Leila could wait. When it was time for her to enter, she had to climb the stairs from the second floor. Her father stood in the back, a solemn expression on his face, waiting for her to emerge so that he could escort her down the aisle. When she appeared at last, resplendent in her white gown, her father's face lit up, and they walked along the red carpet toward me. Leila took her place beside me, and we joined hands.

As Pastor Wu delivered a brief message, I looked out at the congregation. Sitting in the front row were our parents. Our mothers were holding hands. Tears were streaming down Leila's mother's face, and my mom was beaming at me. Beside her, my father sat with his hands folded in his lap, a subtle smile on his lips. I'd heard countless horror stories about arguments between the bride and groom's parents over wedding arrangements, but my parents had simply agreed to go along with Chinese customs.

My dad, who had initially not wanted me to go to China, seemed thankful for the adventure that my path had made possible for all of us. If not for my decision to go into missions, he and my mother might never have climbed the Great Wall or stood among the ranks of terra cotta soldiers that have guarded Emperor Qin's tomb for over two thousand years— and they certainly never would have played such a prominent role in a Chinese wedding.

My eyes returned to Leila, and her smile filled my soul. We spoke our vows in both Chinese and English. We exchanged rings, and then Pastor Wu declared that it was time for me to kiss her. After I had bestowed a timid peck on her lips, he ordered me to kiss her twice more, and everyone laughed. With that, the ceremony was over; we were at last indisputably married in everyone's eyes.

When it came time for the banquet in Leila's hometown, I once again worried about having to drink *baijiu*. By custom at Chinese weddings, the groom is expected to walk around and drink with all of the men, and of course *baijiu* is the required beverage. I talked to Leila about my worry, and she told her father, who agreed to walk around with me and pour sprite into my glass instead of *baijiu*. I was very grateful. For once, I would be able to keep my vow.

The banquet itself was a circus, and Leila and I were the performers. Following the modern tradition, Leila wore three different dresses over the course of the event: a red *qipao*, a Western white wedding dress, and a blue evening gown. At different times, we were whisked onstage, where we presented each other with gifts, recited vows to each other, and poured champagne into a tower of glasses. I sang "I Will Be Here," by Steven Curtis Chapman, which I had translated into Chinese with the help of a friend.

The most important part of the whole ceremony was the *ren qin*, which literally means "recognize relatives." That was the moment when, for the first time, I called Leila's mother "Mom" and her father "Dad." In this manner, I addressed a whole line of relatives, including siblings and aunts and uncles. I spoke to Leila's family in Chinese, and she spoke to mine in English. Thus, my family became hers, and her family became mine.

25

Life Together

One of my favorite pastors in America was fond of quoting the following statistic: Only one out of 1,152 married couples who study their Bibles together get divorced. Although I wondered about the methods that had produced such a suspiciously precise number, I thought that the takeaway lesson was still valid: Regularly studying the Bible with your spouse will strengthen your marriage.

With that in mind, I had been dreaming for years of building a God-centered family on a foundation of daily prayer and Bible study. Now that I was married, I was ready to turn that dream into a reality. Leila was on board, and right from the start we began having daily "quiet times" together on the couch in our living room, our Bibles sitting open in our laps.

During one of those quiet times, Leila brought up the issue that had always troubled her most. "I still don't see how a loving God can send people to hell," she said. It was the same objection I'd had long ago at one of my first Bible studies in college—the objection that had led me to question the existence of hell.

I had come to a point at which I enjoyed pondering such questions. With volumes of apologetics under my belt, I felt confident in my ability to conquer them. Furthermore, as an evangelical, I saw it as my duty to be the spiritual leader in our marriage, and that meant being a teacher. If something about Christianity didn't make sense to my wife, it was my duty to explain it to her. I rose eagerly to her challenge.

In what I now suspect was a sickeningly patronizing tone, I vomited up the stock evangelical answer: It is *we* who have rejected God, not God who has rejected us. Hell is the deserved punishment for people who rebel against their loving creator, I explained. Imagining myself to have answered her question satisfactorily with these words, I turned back to my Bible to move on with our study.

Leila wasn't done, however.

"But God had to know which of us would reject him," she said. "Why would he still create people he knows will reject him—people he knows are destined to spend eternity suffering in hell?" She was now voicing the classic problem of Romans 9. The Apostle Paul himself had agonized over it, and in the end, all he could say was, "Will what is formed say to him who formed it, 'Why did you make me this way?'"

"Don't question God," was what this boiled down to.

It was the answer to so many of the tough questions: God's ways are higher than ours. Deep down, I understood that this was the ultimate cop-out. It was code for, "If it doesn't make sense to you, just stop thinking about it." At the same time, however, God was supposed to be rational. We were supposed to be able to get to know him better by means of study and reason. That was the whole point of theology. We were *not* supposed to stop thinking.

I thought back to the works of John Piper I'd read and struggled to give Leila a more satisfactory answer. Perhaps God was creating people who were destined to go to hell in order to demonstrate his justice. As Piper and so many great theologians before him had concluded, God's ultimate goal was to glorify himself—and the reason this wasn't sinfully narcissistic was that God actually *was* perfect and infinite and therefore *deserved* glory.

Leila was not impressed. She offered another explanation by means of analogy, one that a Bible study leader in college had shared with her: Just as humans choose to have children knowing that some of them may end up leading tragic lives, God still chooses to create us despite his knowledge that some of us will go to hell. He is moved by love to give even the damned a chance to know him.

I thought the analogy sounded pretty good.

But Leila went on to point out the flaw in it: Humans don't have perfect foreknowledge of their children's fates, so it is reasonable for them to roll the dice and hope for a good outcome. But God *knows* the precise fates of all of his children—and so it doesn't make sense to suppose that he harbors hope for those who are destined for destruction.

For the next hour or so, we made our way down a well-traveled path fraught with troubling questions. I continued groping in the dark for answers, but we both only grew more frustrated. Leila was annoyed because I wasn't able to admit that I just didn't have a good explanation. And I was upset because her line of questioning exposed a weakness I had buried long ago, one that undermined the foundation of the Gospel, in which I had chosen to invest my life.

Our conversation ended explosively, and only one thing had been resolved: I was never going to try to "teach" Leila again. Studying the Bible together appeared not to be strengthening our marriage after all, and it was clear that both of us would continue to be bothered by the many disturbing questions that plagued the religion that had brought us together.

Despite such doubts, we continued attending Haidian Church; and we grew *more* involved, not less. Leila joined the translation team, and whenever it was her turn to interpret, we would put on a little radio show for the visiting foreigners who were listening through the receivers that the church provided. As they waited for the service to begin, they would hear us welcoming them to the church and reading and discussing various Bible verses.

The English service was growing. Not only were many

other foreigners involved, but many more locals had stepped in to serve. I helped train people to lead worship on guitar and drums, and it wasn't long before I felt that I was no longer needed. And that was a good thing. Whether or not I could claim any credit, a significant aspect of my mission had been accomplished. Both Leila and I began feeling that it would soon be time to move on, and we decided to apply for a green card.

We knew that getting a green card could take up to three years; and so as we waited, we had to get on with our lives. Leila took a job with an interior design firm that renovated and furnished corporate office buildings, and I accepted a job as a physics teacher at the Beijing World Youth Academy. These were steps up for both of us, and for the most part, we were satisfied with the prospect of making the most of our remaining time in Beijing.

I remained involved in church, attending Bible studies and often leading worship. But I was slowly growing more frustrated with God. All of the great promises in the Bible, which I wanted to take at face value, seemed to be worth very little in practice. The entire field of theology was beginning to seem like an unending exercise in fabricating excuses for why God just didn't seem to be doing anything.

When people were seriously ill, we would pray for them, but we knew that they would have to be treated by a doctor in order to get well. And if you looked around at all the people who were being fervently prayed for, their chances of getting well just happened to be exactly what you would expect based on ordinary statistics alone.

Regarding prayer for other matters—for peace in a warring country, financial provision for people in need, salvation for unbelievers—I felt that the results also appeared patently equivalent to what would have happened without prayer. Some conflicts were resolved, some not. Some people had their needs met, some didn't. Some nonbelievers came to Christ—but very few.

Why could I not see God working?

My last-ditch effort to answer this question was to suppose that God hides his works for profound reasons. If you can't see his hand in the world, it's because you're blinded by your unbelief. And even if you believe, you still won't be able to see his work because God doesn't *want* us to rely on evidence; he wants us to have *faith*. I was beginning to recognize these "answers" as rationalizations made up by someone who was desperate to keep believing despite a total lack of evidence.

All of these questions were on my mind when I walked into a bookstore in Kuala Lumpur, where I was attending a conference for teachers. There on the shelf of new releases was a copy of *God Is Not Great*, by Christopher Hitchens. In the past, I had only read books about Christianity that were written by Christians. But at that moment, I decided that if my basis for belief was truly strong, my faith could stand up to whatever attacks might be leveled against it in a book. So I bought it.

It was, of course, a foolish decision to pick up that book: I was tempting Satan. But part of me recognized that this sort of thought was just another mechanism people use to shut down their minds and cling to something that they know deep down isn't really true. In any case, I was already asking the big questions myself, and it wouldn't be Christopher Hitchens' fault if, after reading his book, I gave up my faith.

I almost did.

Few of Hitchens' arguments were new to me; they were the same questions that had plagued me from the beginning. He just helped me to recognize the tenuous nature of the mental gymnastics that I'd been performing in order to keep the whole house of cards from collapsing. When I finished the book, I posted a review on Amazon in which I attempted to rebut his arguments; but it was really myself that I was trying to convince.

Still, I was not ready to give up, and there were a handful of threads that I clung to—the same threads to which I had been returning for years. One was the martyrdom of the saints, who had presumably died for their beliefs. Surely, these people—who had either witnessed a genuine resurrection or knew it to be false—would not have died for a lie. There was also the evidence of transformed lives. My brother's life, and his whole attitude, had been transformed when he became a believer. So had my own. And finally, what of the powerful experience I'd had after praying to receive Christ as my savior so many years ago? Surely these things proved that God was there, I told myself.

I knew, though, that even these arguments were weak. After all, there were martyrs in other faiths who also ought not to have died knowingly for a lie. Why should such martyrdom count as evidence for Christianity but not for other religions? And similarly, plenty of people experienced equally dramatic transformations after converting to other faiths. Again, if such transformations counted as legitimate evidence for Christianity, then the same was true for other faiths. The same went for powerful emotional experiences at the moment of conversion. None of my last-ditch arguments really indicated that there was anything unique about Christianity.

I ultimately fell back on the final, most desperate recourse of all: If I was to continue believing, I could appeal only to faith itself. I was forced to suppose that these apparent shortcomings of Christianity and contradictions about God and the Bible must be resolved in some higher plane of understanding, and I simply had to accept that I would never have access to this higher plane during my life on earth.

Time passed, and as Leila and I wrapped up our final commitments in Beijing, my faith suffered another blow. My father told me that a friend of his was dying from brain cancer. He had already had an operation, but the cancer had returned and spread quickly. The situation looked grim. For the first time ever, my father was asking me for prayer. My faith had long since shrunk to the size of a mustard seed, but that was supposed to be enough for God; so I prayed anyway. But just a few days later, my father's friend died.

It was yet another reminder that God's decisions about when to cure sick people matched up suspiciously well—perfectly, in fact—with the natural laws of probability. Take breast cancer for instance. If the survival rate a hundred years ago was only, say, one percent, then it would have just so happened that one percent of breast cancer patients who received prayer would be healed. And as modern medicine brought the survival rate up to eighty percent, it now happened that eighty percent of those who received prayer were healed.

I tried to make myself believe that this was actually a sign of God's awesome omnipotence. He was able to carry out his will and his miracles while remaining mysterious in his ways and allowing nature to appear to run its course according to the simple laws of nature that we observed experimentally. What sovereignty! But, I wondered, is there even a difference between a god who hides himself so perfectly and no god at all?

I had been in Beijing for five years now. I had wanted to be an instrument through which God might carry out his mighty work. He was supposed to be great enough to bring about big changes through small people. But all that really changed was my understanding of the world—God, China, my own faith, and intercultural relations. More than anything else, I felt disillusioned. Before boarding the plane to return to America, I wrote the following entry in my journal:

> Since trying and failing to fit into Chinese culture, I've finally realized how truly difficult it is to assimilate in a foreign country, especially one that's so thoroughly different from your own. Now I understand the difficulty experienced by Chinese people in America.

Above all else, I've learned that building bridges is hard work. Sometimes I see myself as a martyr, a soldier in one of the first waves of attacks on the stronghold of misunderstanding. In my lifetime, there will be misunderstandings and uncomfortable stares and miscommunications—but perhaps future generations will have a better experience as a result my generation's work.

In a way, we all have the option to be martyrs in this sense. We cannot attain a perfect world within our lifetime, but we can all hope to make some small improvements that will be enjoyed by future generations. We can choose to live for ourselves, without a care for the future, leaving posterity to take care of itself, or we can give up our own desires to make the world a better place for those who will come after us.

Most of us probably never realize that everything in life that we enjoy—the freedom, the convenience, and technology of the modern age—is a result of hard work done over hundreds of past generations. Sometimes only tiny steps were made from one generation to the next, but over time those steps added up to give us the world as we experience it today. And we take this for granted.

What these words revealed was that my own understanding of my mission had changed over that five-year period. Whereas I had initially come in hopes of converting people to my religion, I had ended up focusing on tearing down cultural barriers and promoting harmonious relations instead. The reason for this change was something that I didn't want to face, something I couldn't bring myself to write, even in my private journal: My faith was dying.

26

Tribulation

My first big shock after returning to Houston was that I got sunburned in only twenty minutes while we were moving into our new apartment. I took it as a good sign: It meant that the air was clean enough for sunlight to pass through it. In Beijing, the smog had always been so thick that I could spend hours outside without even turning pink.

The second big shock was that Leila had breast cancer. When she found the lumps, everyone assured her that they would turn out to be benign. After all, she was only twenty-seven years old, and who got breast cancer at that age? But after a few doctor's appointments and one quick phone call, she was sobbing in my arms, asking how much time she had left to live.

We had just begun building a new life together. I was teaching math at a private high school, while she was taking prerequisites for a nursing program. She had wanted to work in the field of medicine ever since she was a little girl; but in China, she had been forced into an engineering major that she never liked. Our move to America had been her chance to make a fresh start.

We had also joined a church. Despite my nagging doubts about God, I had felt that one of the most important orders of business was to find a community of believers. I just couldn't imagine life otherwise. We had visited an evangelical Chinese church on the recommendation of a friend and found the people there genial and welcoming—so we made it our home.

After receiving Leila's diagnosis, we turned to our friends there for support. One of them prayed that Leila's cancer would eventually be no more than a blip in our life history. And everyone prayed for her healing, often inserting the habitual qualifier, "if it's your will, Lord." That was the escape hatch that Christians were always careful to leave open for God in case our prayers weren't granted. And I knew the probability that God would need to use it.

Leila had a high-grade, triple-negative, invasive ductal carcinoma that had metastasized to six lymph nodes on her left side. A little research revealed that the standard treatment would give her roughly a three-in-four chance of beating it. Not bad odds if you're gambling for a few bucks—but nothing you would ever want to stake your life on.

The first week had involved nothing but tests. But we had yet to find an oncologist and begin a course of treatment. When I called the hospital to make an appointment and get these things going, the woman I spoke to took Leila's insurance information and said that she would call me back in a few minutes.

As I waited, I thought about our situation and told myself that everything would be fine. I had lived in China for five years with no insurance at all. Knowing that that was just asking for trouble, I had been careful to obtain policies for both of us as soon as we moved to America. I felt confident that we would be taken care of if disaster struck.

When the woman called back, she told me that Leila's insurance would not cover her treatment. A clause in the fine print of the policy limited coverage of outpatient services to $2,500; and as it turned out, nearly every component of cancer treatment counted as an outpatient service. It was a hell of a time for me to learn how insurance policies worked.

While I was still trying to process everything the woman had just said, she asked me, "Do you still want to keep the appointment tomorrow?" It seemed a ridiculous question; surely we could receive treatment and work out the financial details later.

I asked how much everything was likely to cost, expecting to hear a number somewhere between twenty thousand and forty thousand dollars. *Maybe* fifty or sixty thousand at most. So her answer shocked me. She rattled off what was apparently their standard estimate for breast cancer patients:

anywhere from $114,000 to $264,000 in the first year. Then, for emphasis, she repeated that that was *just the first year.*

My heart turned to ice. That was far beyond what we were capable of handling. How could treatment *possibly* be that expensive? And was it necessary to consider the cost for an entire *year* of treatment? Couldn't we just take things one step at a time? I asked about expenses for the first week.

The lady informed me that we would have to pay $21,855 up front just to get in the door. She also warned that once we paid that amount, we might be denied any financial assistance because the very fact that we *had* paid that much would be seen as evidence that we had no need—even if the payment exhausted our entire savings.

She repeated her earlier question: Did I want to keep the appointment for tomorrow? She sounded eager to get me off the phone, as if she were paid by the number of clients she talked to each day. But I needed to think. Everything she had just told me pointed to an obvious answer: No. But what then? How much cheaper could cancer treatment be elsewhere?

Then a bell rang in my head. She had said the words "financial assistance." I asked her about it, and she gave me some phone numbers for various programs, which I began calling immediately. They all had a series of questions that they went through; and there was always one question that disqualified us.

"Is your wife a U.S. citizen?"
"No."

"I'm sorry, she doesn't qualify."

"What's your annual household income?"
"Forty-two thousand dollars."
"I'm sorry, that's too high. You don't qualify."

"How long has your wife had her green card?"
"One year."
"I'm sorry, she doesn't qualify."

I tried every number the lady had given me, but each call ended the same way. That quickly, all the options were gone, and I was back where I'd started. We had enough money for the first appointment. We would even have some money left over. But before long, we would be broke. What then?

I thought back to a time in Beijing when I had helped someone in need. Our church there had a member who had developed a brain aneurism. She needed 100,000 kuai for an operation (about $14,000). She would certainly die soon otherwise. Her husband was crippled and living in the Philippines. She had come to China for better work opportunities and was supporting her family from Beijing.

I had never met the woman, but I wanted to help. The cost of 100,000 kuai seemed enormous to me at the time. I certainly wasn't rich, but as a foreign teacher in China, I was enjoying a low cost of living and had been able to save some money. When thinking about how much to give, the first number that came to mind was 5,000 kuai—about $625.

I called the pastor who was in charge of collecting donations and arranged to meet him at a hotel. I got there early and waited in a courtyard by a fountain. It was dark and cold—the middle of winter. When he arrived, I handed him an envelope with 5,000 kuai in it. I saw that he was tired, and I knew that he was the only one looking after this woman with the aneurism. I imagined it had put some strain on his family, so I gave him another 300 kuai and told him to use it to cover his own expenses in the ordeal. He burst into tears and nearly collapsed into my arms, hugging me tightly, unable to say a word.

That experience had felt wonderful. At the time, I thought that maybe someday I would need help, too; and now that day had arrived. I wondered whether anyone would reach out to help us as I had done to help that woman.

I called my dad and recounted all the phone calls I had just made, quoting the numbers. He wasn't surprised that Leila didn't qualify for assistance. He reminded me that when we applied for Leila's green card, we had been required to guarantee that she would not become dependent on government aid.

"Keep the appointment," he said. "I'll help you cover the cost." Then he added, "She's my daughter." He was reminding me of the *ren qin* ceremony at our wedding, and as soon as he spoke those words, I began sobbing uncontrollably—just like that pastor I'd helped in Beijing.

I kept the appointment, and after a few further tests, Leila had been prescribed a course of treatment: six months of chemotherapy, followed by surgery and radiation. Her first chemo treatment was on Good Friday—the start of Easter weekend, five years after we had met while waiting in line outside of Haidian Church in Beijing.

When our friends at church learned about the inadequacy of Leila's insurance policy, they were eager to help. One guy in my Bible study, Steve, offered to organize a benefit concert. He had managed a similar fundraiser before and was a gifted administrator.

I felt guilty just thinking about it. For one thing, I didn't like having to ask for help; and for another, I was arriving at a point where I wasn't sure I even believed in God anymore. But it was Leila that mattered; and perhaps through the church's provision for us, my faith could be revived. I accepted Steve's offer, imagining a small event at which I might play the piano and sing a few Chinese songs.

Steve recruited others to help and called a meeting to lay out our vision for the concert. My dad accompanied me. One of the first orders of business was to set a goal. It raised an uncomfortable question: How much money did I want other people to give us?

My dad and I looked at each other. We hadn't talked about it. I thought about the range that the lady at the hospital had given me. If the total cost ended up being in the middle of that range and I paid as much as I could and then split the remainder between my dad and our supporters, we would need about $50,000. In one sense, it sounded like an unreasonably huge amount. But in the context of cancer treatment, it was really quite small. I whispered the number to my dad with a questioning eyebrow raised. He nodded, and that was the goal we set.

A lot happened over the next few months. Leila's body was ravaged by the chemotherapy. Her hair fell out, and she went into chemically-induced menopause. After her weekly dosages—each of which cost a few thousand dollars—I would often hold her while she vomited into the toilet. I remember seeing a warning label on the IV bag saying that whoever handled it must wear gloves and be careful not to allow it to contact their skin since it was poisonous. And yet, they were pumping it directly into my wife's veins.

I changed jobs, signing on to teach at the high school from which I had graduated. It had a supportive community, and working there would enable me to get decent health insurance for Leila—though her cancer would count as a preexisting condition, and the first year of treatment would not be covered. Still, it was better than any of the options that were available through my current job. Our immediate financial need didn't change, though.

The concert took place in the fall of 2010, and it shaped up to be a big event. The first half consisted of performances by church members, including myself—I played Chopin's *Fantaisie-Impromptu* and Beethoven's *Moonlight Sonata*— and the second half included performances by a professional dance group, an acting troupe, and a local Christian singer.

When the concert was just wrapping up, I ran into one of the men who had helped organize it, a guy named Yates.

He was standing like a pillar outside the doors to the sanctuary, watching with a contemplative expression on his face. From his shoulder hung a non-descript black bag. He saw me out of the corner of his eye and then turned toward me, smiling. His posture and his voice radiated peace. "This is good for the church," he said.

Those were words that I needed to hear. Leila and I had benefitted so much from the church. We'd seen the people give their time; we had received money from them; and now the church was lending its facilities for the concert. I felt guilty about being such a huge burden. To hear that the community that had sacrificed so much for us was benefitting from the experience relieved me of that guilt.

Yates then patted the bag and said, "It's all here."

I knew what he meant. All of the donations were in the bag. I hadn't even known that Yates was going to be in charge of gathering the money, but it made sense. I didn't know anyone more trustworthy than him. He handed me the bag, and I took Leila home.

That night, I was up until 3:00 a.m. counting and documenting all of the donations. When I finished, I sat there, exhausted, looking at the total amount. Including the substantial donations that had been made during the weeks before the concert, it all added up to $50,102.46. We had hit our goal right on the nose. Leila wrote the following note of thanks to everyone in our community:

It was a MIRACLE! That's all I can say about the

concert on Saturday night. Thank you for helping to make it possible. When I look in the mirror, I see a girl who couldn't be more ordinary. But God's love and your support have made me feel that I'm special and precious. Thank you for your kindness, generosity, and love. Thank you for standing with me.

The precision with which we hit our fundraising goal was remarkable, and I was conditioned by my years in the evangelical community to interpret it as clear evidence of the hand of God. But there was a war being waged within me. Part of me was asking, "If God really cares so much, why let Leila get cancer in the first place?" The answer, of course, was that it was part of his plan. We might never know the reason in this life, but ultimately her suffering would result in some greater good.

The remainder of the year was filled with even more miracles of God's provision. He provided Leila with heroic strength to persevere in her studies throughout her courses of chemotherapy and radiation treatment. Even after her surgery, when she had a drainage tube protruding from her side, connected to a fluid collection bulb that had to be emptied twice a day, she continued attending her classes.

When she was broadsided by an SUV on the way to her radiation treatment and our car was totaled, a church member and a neighbor let us borrow their cars during the time it took us to get a replacement.

When a man who had been indicted for his wife's murder

but was currently out on bail acquired partial ownership of our apartment complex and filed to have us evicted, the mother of one of my students contacted me and offered us a free place to stay—for years, if we needed it. The timing was perfect, and it was in an ideal location, so we accepted the offer.

When it was announced that my school would have to lay off one teacher from each department and that the most recent hires were the most vulnerable, I applied and was accepted into the graduate physics program at Rice University. Without the free place to stay, it would not have been financially feasible for me to go to graduate school just as Leila was preparing to attend nursing school.

The year had been filled with challenges, but at every step, God had been there to provide us with exactly what we needed in order to prevail. At least, that's what I wanted to believe. I had been hoping that all of the blessings we experienced would reignite my faith. But that's not what happened.

Testimonies even more powerful than my own are common among all religions—Islam, Judaism, Mormonism, and more. The fact that we had been provided for proved that the people at our church genuinely cared about us; but I had to admit that it said nothing about the truth of Christian *doctrine*. Moreover, I was keenly aware that there were others whose needs were just as great and whose prayers were just as fervent who were *not* provided for.

When a lone man survives a fiery crash that leaves others dead, he is likely to say that it was God who saved him. He points to his own survival as evidence for the grace of God. The deceased victims are often conveniently ignored. For some hidden reason, God's grace did not extend to them.

It was tempting to call our experience miraculous, and I did so at the time. But deep down, I was aware that there were perfectly natural explanations for it all. The people around us were loving and kind. Leila and I were the lucky ones. What about the many good Christian women who were dying of breast cancer in countries where effective treatment simply wasn't available? Where was the miracle they needed?

My faith in God was nearly dead, but my love for the Church remained strong. It had done so much for us that I simply couldn't abandon it. I remained heavily involved, and I began playing the piano and drums in the worship band. Occasionally I would even lead on guitar. But I was becoming keenly aware that my thoughts and prayers no longer matched the official doctrine of the church.

Inside, I felt tortured.

27

Unborn Again

It was the middle of the night, and I found myself sitting up in bed, panting, covered in sweat. I wasn't sure whether I had been sleeping fitfully or had never fallen asleep in the first place. That wasn't really an important question, though, because at the moment I was certain that I was about to die.

My heart was racing, and there was a painful tightness in my chest. It was different from what I had felt in that middle school locker room after gym class twenty years earlier, when I had first become frightened about my heart and promised God that I would become a minister. And it was different from an episode of atrial fibrillation I'd recently experienced.

I wondered whether this might be a heart attack.

Reason told me that this was unlikely. I was only thirty-one years old, and my cholesterol level had always been excellent, as well as my blood pressure. I was in good shape and exercised regularly. *It's just a panic attack,* I thought. *It has to be.*

Careful not to wake Leila, I got up and Googled the symptoms of a heart attack. Then I did the same for panic attacks. There was a lot of overlap, and what I was experiencing seemed to fit either one equally well. But surely a panic attack was far more probable. A heart attack would be about as likely as . . . *What? A twenty-seven-year-old girl getting breast cancer?*

I took an aspirin, thinking that it might help just in case. And in an effort to calm myself, I picked up Bella, a fluffy little terrier we had recently acquired, and carried her around the room for a while. I closed my eyes and breathed slowly. After ten or twenty minutes, I felt almost normal again, though I was a bit shaky and raw—the way you feel right after narrowly avoiding a catastrophic collision on the freeway.

That I felt better seemed like evidence that it had, in fact, been nothing but a panic attack. I slipped back into bed, but I was still gripped by fear. What if it came back? And what if it wasn't a panic attack, but rather the first small rumblings of something much worse? Lying in bed, I could feel every beat of my heart, and after each one, I was terrified that the next would never come.

In the morning, I told Leila about it. She knew something about panic attacks from her nursing studies, and she said that if I had indeed had one, I was likely to have more. It turned out that she was right. Later that morning, it happened again—when I was driving. I told myself that it was just another panic attack; but almost by definition, someone who's having a panic attack finds it difficult to believe that that's all it is.

Maybe this is it, I thought. *Maybe I'm going to die now.*

It occurred to me that if I *was* about to die, it would at least be minimally thoughtful for me to pull my car into a parking lot and politely die outside of the flow of traffic. Otherwise, I would cause a traffic jam at best—and get someone else killed at worst. So I turned into a parking lot, stopped my car, and tried to calm myself again. After several minutes, the sensation passed, and I once more felt reassured that it was only a panic attack.

In the following days, I tried to forget about the attacks and get on with my life; but then my heart really did start acting up again. And this time I was sure of it—there were palpitations, skipped beats, and episodes of fluttering—so I decided to see a doctor.

The cardiologist said that my heart was in good shape. My symptoms could all be caused by lack of sleep, dehydration, too much caffeine, or—of course—stress. I should examine my habits and my circumstances and make adjustments where I could. He asked whether I had any unusual sources of stress in my life.

Well, who didn't?

I was now a full year into graduate school, and my studies weren't easy. And although more than a year and a half had passed since Leila's last treatment, I worried about her constantly. There were just too many stories about cancer survivors whose illness returned in an incurable form. Somehow, though, I felt certain that these things weren't the root of my problem.

It was impossible to know for sure, of course, what was really behind the panic attacks and palpitations; but what had been bothering me most over the past few months was my involvement at church and the status of my faith. I had been leading the congregation in singing lyrics that no longer seemed true to me. In the beginning, I had been singing with genuine hope that they *were* true. But as time passed, that hope had faded.

I now felt like a hypocrite.

The cognitive dissonance was becoming unbearable, and I had to get out. I had to step down from my role in the praise band; but I didn't want to rock the boat. I didn't want to discourage or shock anyone with the news that I was losing my faith. So I took the easy way out: I called the pastor and told him that I needed to step down for health reasons. It was the truth, but it wasn't the whole truth. Fortunately, nobody asked any questions, and I quietly slipped into the shadows.

After that, I kept attending church, and I continued praying—but more out of a sense of obligation than anything else. During sermons, I found myself thinking that the whole foundation beneath each message was a lie. And when it came time to pray, the only words I could utter were, "Lord, thank you for Leila." Nothing else would come out.

I made the conscious decision to expand my reading. Throughout my Christian life, most of my information about the opposing viewpoints had come to me filtered through the writings of Christian apologists. The few times that I deviated from this rule, I had caught glimpses of the illusion of my own faith as viewed from the outside—and I had seen hints of greater truths and greater mysteries than what were accessible from within the evangelical bubble.

Now I was finally interested in finding truth for truth's sake rather than merely searching for evidence to buttress propositions that I was desperate to validate. The more I read, and the more I thought, the more I realized the questions that had been building in my mind over the years had no truly satisfying answers. I had been willing to accept unsatisfying answers simply because I had *wanted* my beliefs to be true.

It was now time, I decided, to discard that bias.

My inquiry led me to the conclusion that an honest examination of any one of a number of academic subjects—history, geology, cosmology, biology, or anthropology, to name a few—revealed that the Bible did not give an accurate account of the history of the world or the development of human civilization. And so, from the outset, a prospective Christian must either reject clear evidence and proceed on blind faith—which could just as easily be applied to any other religion with the same validity—or assume that the Bible was largely metaphorical.

I also began to look at the Bible itself with fresh eyes. What I saw was that the power, character, and morality of the

---

god portrayed within it never exceeded the capacity of the imaginations of the people who were writing about him at the time. It was a funny coincidence, I thought, that as people have become more civilized, so has God himself. This does not seem to be evidence for an immutable god whose goodness transcends human understanding, but a manmade myth who is limited by the extent of his creators' knowledge.

I began to feel appalled by the actions of the god of the Old Testament. On many occasions, he commanded his people to slaughter entire societies, sparing not even the animals. The theological excuse that I had once accepted, but which now seemed shamefully flimsy to me, was that these societies had rejected their creator and were committing idolatry. If the Israelites had let them survive, Israel itself would have been polluted by their idolatry; so they had to go.

But was bloody extermination really the best solution that a loving, merciful, all-powerful god could contrive? This was supposed to be the same god who concocted the grandest redemption scheme in all of history, who was so bent on saving the Lost that he sent his son to die an excruciating death on a cross. Where were his love and redemption at the time of Noah or Joshua? The obvious answer was that God's love had not yet been fleshed out by the people who were inventing him.

Was it more reasonable to assume that these other societies truly deserved to be victims of genocide because of their unwitting rejection of their creator, or that Yahweh's commands to slaughter them were actually fabricated by leaders among the Israelites to rally the troops and rationalize their actions? It was now evident to me that the latter view made more sense and reflected human actions that were typical of tribal societies throughout history.

Not only was I now beginning to see God as immoral, but I also realized that he was obsessed with some absurdly arbitrary pet peeves. These resulted in an entire book of laws about what people were allowed to eat, how they were to conduct animal sacrifices, what kinds of fiber were acceptable for making cloth, and on which days of the week people were allowed to pick fruit.

Previously, I had thought that such laws were in place to protect us from diseases and other ills that people simply did not understand at the time. But if that was truly the case, why was God more concerned with laying down petty rules than with providing revelations that might actually help us understand and cure the diseases? Again, the nature of God's concerns seemed to be a hallmark of the limitations of the people who were creating him. And on the whole, I had to admit that it made little sense for a god of truly cosmic proportions to be concerned with such mundane and arbitrary matters.

God was supposed to be omnipotent, but I now saw in the Bible a deity whose power was severely limited. If it had really been the *humans* who bothered God in the time of Noah, why couldn't he have devised a way to exterminate them without wastefully destroying *all* animal life on earth? Or better yet, why couldn't he have gotten creation right on the first try, making both the Flood and the Crucifixion—not to mention hell—unnecessary? And then, of course, there was the embarrassing passage in Judges, where it says that God "could not drive out the inhabitants of the valley, because they had chariots of iron." If God had trouble with chariots of iron, then he would probably shit his heavenly pants at the sight of a nuclear submarine.

Yahweh didn't really come across as omniscient, either. Why should he have to test people to find out whether they were truly devoted to him? Why has he been so embarrassingly silent about things that an omniscient God would have known about our universe, which we know now? It has been too convenient a coincidence for theologians that God reveals knowledge about our universe only after we happen to discover it on our own.

God was also inconsistent, often changing his mind or allowing himself to be persuaded by men. In Genesis, God was persuaded by Abraham not to destroy Sodom. And in Exodus, God "was about to kill" Moses but decided to "let him alone" after Moses' wife circumcised their son. What, I wondered, was God's purpose in such interactions? If he was really in control of everything, as when he hardened Pharaoh's heart, he appeared to have been amusing himself with a game of chess—against himself—in which real people suffered as a result.

How loving was that?

On top of all of it all, I was beginning to see God as a terrible planner, woefully lacking in foresight. If, as Genesis suggests, humanity was the pinnacle of creation, then the whole scheme was poorly thought out and terribly inefficient. Why create a million billion billion stars and guide life along a multi-billion-year evolution process on just one particular planet orbiting one particular star, allowing 99% of all species to go extinct along the way—all for one particular species of ape?

Even God's plan of redemption was poorly conceived. If he intended from the very beginning to redeem sinners via Christ's sacrifice, why destroy the unrighteous with a flood earlier on? Why keep sending prophets to continually threaten his people with destruction if they didn't repent? And finally, why distribute the vehicle of redemption—the Gospel—so unequally, so that only people who were fortunate to have been born in the right time and place had a chance at salvation?

A truly universal God, if discoverable at all, ought to be discoverable to *anyone*, on *any* continent (or planet, for that matter), at *any* time in history. And yet each of the Judeo-Christian sects contains at its core the belief that its founding was the result of a unique revelation given at a select moment in history to a chosen individual who was part of a favored group of people who happened to speak God's preferred language. In light of all that we now know about history, such a proposition simply seems utterly ridiculous. I had once been able to respond to this with the words of Tertullian, saying, "I believe because it is absurd."

But not anymore.

What, then, was to become of my faith?

I could not be a New-Testament-only Christian and dismiss the horrors of the Old Testament, saying, "All of that has been replaced by the New Covenant, so it's not relevant." For according to the New Testament itself, the god who sent Jesus to share his wisdom and die for our sins was the same god who flooded the earth, slaughtered the Egyptian firstborn, and commanded his people to commit genocide. To admit that the character of the god described in the Old Testament was abhorrent while at the same time believing wholeheartedly in Christ as the fulfillment of the Old Testament god's ultimate plan was to concede from the outset that God himself was inconsistent and that huge parts of the Bible were entirely invalid. The essence of the New Testament—the Gospel—depended strongly on the truth of the Old Testament. Either both were true, or both were false.

Nor could I be satisfied with simply reinterpreting the scriptures, as liberal theologians are apt to do. Many of them would say that God is more nuanced and more sophisticated than what I have been describing. Of *course* the Bible is not intended to be taken literally. Of *course* the ugly parts—such as those advocating genocide—don't reflect God's true character. But such an approach leaves us with two problems: First, how do we know which parts are to be taken metaphorically? And second, how do we know which parts do not accurately reflect the character of God?

Both of these questions present us with a continuous spectrum from "all of scripture" to "none of it." And at each point on this spectrum, an entire school of theology can be found. The only way to investigate which one is correct is by examining the writings of other theologians or by weighing the scriptures with one's own conscience. In either case, we are ultimately appealing to the opinions of other fallible humans, and we end up with a subjectively judged, relativistic moral philosophy and a faith that may be "true" for one person but not true for another—a result that is completely indistinguishable from what we would get by using our own conscience to develop our system of morals in the first place, independent of any scriptures.

This simply would not do.

The Christianity that I had known for so long now seemed unsalvageable. In my efforts to scrutinize it, I had gotten too close, and the whole edifice had vanished like a mirage. The very questions that had plagued me from the beginning had snowballed, crushing my faith entirely. If I was to go on believing in anything, my only option seemed to be to look elsewhere for a more palatable god, one worthy of worship. But I could only embrace such a god if there appeared to be compelling evidence for its existence—and I could now find no such evidence.

These developments in my thinking unfolded over a period of a year or more. And at the end of it all, I realized I had become something that I had previously thought abominable: an atheist. But I was different from what I had always assumed atheists to be. I didn't hate God. I wasn't angry at him, and I wasn't leaving the faith in order to pursue an immoral, hedonistic lifestyle. In fact, I wasn't rejecting God by choice at all.

I was simply no longer *able* to believe.

I *wish* there were a benevolent, omnipotent God who cared to take an interest in our affairs. I *wish* that we could all be set free from our own destructive impulses. I *wish* that we could spend eternity in a paradise filled with love and joy beyond anything we can imagine in this life. Who would not want these things? But *wanting* them to be true does not *make* them true. This was a sad admission for me to make.

There remained many things that I loved about Christianity: the Golden Rule; the exhortation not to judge others; the importance of helping those in need; the sense that everything you have is a gift and that even the virtues of your own character are the result of forces beyond your control. If we all took these teachings to heart, I believe the world would be a better place.

But these values are not unique to Christianity, and they were ultimately not enough to keep me going to church. So one day, I simply stopped attending. I let go of the tenets of faith that had been the centerpiece of my life for so many years. The biblical account of creation, the fall of man, and redemption through Christ—in short, the Gospel—are, upon honest inspection, myths. The proposition that you deserve to go to hell doesn't even make sense because there is, in fact, no hell.

And *that* is good news.